MW00629395

Praise for *Special Needs Parenting*

Intelligent and incisive, compassionate and empathic, Lorna Bradley's book speaks into the heart of all who want to "love our neighbor as ourselves"— especially when that neighbor is someone who deals on a daily basis with a special needs child. An authentic and realistic look into the challenges of raising children with special needs combined with a message of hope and abundance.

Rev. Dr. Libby Vincent
Adjunct Professor of Systematic Theology, Fuller Theological Seminary

Written from the crucible of her heart, Lorna masterfully leads parents through the emotional roller coaster many feel as they navigate this uncharted territory, and helps them name the feelings that simmer below the surface. And with naming comes healing.

Rev. Leslie Neugent
PARABLES Ministry, Wayzata Community Church

Lorna Bradley's book for families with special needs is a must for the church. Here parents, Christian educators, and pastors can find hard-won wisdom and practical guidance for parenting and providing loving ministry for families with special needs. Bradley is a practitioner of everything she describes. Her writing is clear, accessible, and honest.

Rev. Elaine A. Heath, PhD
McCreless Professor of Evangelism, Perkins School of Theology

Bradley's words "encouraging special needs parents is at the heart of my calling in ministry" is evident on every page. The mother of a son on the autism spectrum, Bradley writes from her personal experience, pastoral grounding in scripture, doctoral studies, and extensive experience leading groups for parents of children with special needs.

Kathleen Deyer Bolduc
Author of The Spiritual Art of Raising Children with Disabilities
and Autism & Alleluias

Families impacted by disability will treasure this study guide because it provides an avenue to help them process the emotional roller coaster of life with special needs. *Special Needs Parenting* offers stories, scripture, and tools for self-care and maintaining healthy relationships. It transcends pain and loss and becomes inspirational.

Jennifer Ross
Special Needs Director, UM Church of the Resurrection

What participants are saying

The small group meetings for *Special Needs Parenting* were timely for my wife and me as we were going through a bit of drama and uncertainty with our teenage daughter. We were able to get the moral and spiritual support we needed from the group. Although each parent has a child with different needs, the needs of the parents are the same—the need to know that you are not alone. This small group stands out as a real blessing.

Robert and Tina Reid

I was impressed by Lorna's research and the materials she created to empower special needs parents. As familiarity developed, the group became attached and supportive of one another. Lorna's focus on how spirituality can aid and empower parents was an important part of each session. I left each meeting more informed and equipped with tools to enhance my life and hopefully lives of others around me.

Michelle Bain

I really enjoyed sharing my perspective candidly with the group and benefited greatly being able to hear others felt the same way. The open candor of everyone was refreshing. Being able to look at our situations from a spiritual perspective was as important to Traci and me as much as the sharing with other parents.

David and Traci Croke

Lorna's book focuses on topics that special needs parents experience every day, but that are often ignored because of the unique challenges we face as parents—topics like grief, self-care, and healthy relationships. Although the children of our group members had different diagnoses, Lorna's book linked our common concerns and experiences that led to sharing, connections, and personal growth.

Kelsey Skiba

Special Needs Parenting is full of thoughtful reflections and personal stories from the author's own journey of parenting a child with special needs. Like an expert guide, Lorna leads the reader down the path of understanding and acceptance, through the twists and turns of loss and loneliness, ultimately arriving at a place of peace and hope. I came away with the wonderful reassurance that Jesus knows what I am going through, and that he genuinely cares for me and for my child.

Suzanne Werlein

special needs

PARENTING

ABOUT THE COVER

There is a style of Japanese art called *Kintsugi*, which means "beautifully broken." It is broken pottery that has been repaired with seams of pure gold. These amazing creations of beauty from brokenness make it clear that perfection is overrated. Real beauty comes from embracing the twists and turns of a unique journey where God is ever present, pouring God's love and grace into the broken places. Where God pours in the gold, we are made all the stronger.

Antique Chinese cup restored by Morty Bachar, Lakeside Pottery

special needs
PARENTING

from coping to thriving

LORNA BRADLEY

FOREWORD BY ERIK CARTER, PhD

MINNEAPOLIS

© 2015 Lorna Bradley
Publishing consultant: Huff Publishing Associates, www.huffpublishing.com, Minneapolis.

Funding and research development support provided by the Hope and Healing Institute, www.hopeandhealingcenter.org.

Hope&Healing

ISBN: 978-0-9908073-2-2

Manufactured in the United States of America

DEDICATION

To my husband, Mark, for your love, encouragement,
and for always holding my hand when we scuba dive.

To my son, Craig, for your courage and determination.
You inspire me every day.

To the parents of extraordinary children.
You are not alone.

TABLE OF CONTENTS

FOREWORD

We were never meant to walk alone.

Along life's journey, our pathways are rarely predictable. Great joys and deep challenges mingle in unanticipated ways. Ordinary experiences are interrupted by the extraordinary that catch us by surprise. Plans we lay out for ourselves don't always materialize as we hoped. Parents know this ebb and flow well. Parents of children with special needs perhaps know it best.

These parents were not meant to walk alone.

More than one in four families in the United States has a member with a disability.[1] Millions of families living in every community across the country include a son or daughter with special needs—children with diagnoses like autism, Down syndrome, learning disabilities, health impairments, and many others. The faith of these parents—and the relationships they develop with others—can provide a rich source of strength and support as they navigate the joys and challenges of raising a child with a disability.[2] What might it look like to support these families well?

In this compelling book, Lorna Bradley offers parents three wonderful gifts.

---

1   G. T. Fujiura, "The Political Arithmetic of Disability and the American Family: A Demographic Perspective," *Family Relations*, 63, (2014): 7–19.

2   T. L. Boehm, E. W. Carter, and J. L. Taylor (in press), "Factors Associated with Family Quality of Life during the Transition to Adulthood for Youth and Young Adults with Developmental Disabilities," *American Journal on Intellectual and Developmental Disabilities*.

First, her seven-part study of Scripture assures parents they are never alone on this journey. Never. God is present—without exception or footnote. God's faithfulness is never challenged or diminished by the presence of a disability. And God's enduring love provides a firm foundation.

Second, Lorna invites parents to walk alongside one another, hand in hand. Although this study can certainly be undertaken alone, something remarkable happens when parents gather together regularly to reflect on their common journey. They find and give encouragement, empathy, friendship, confidence, and grace. As stories are shared, ideas exchanged, tears shed, prayers offered, and love dispensed, a new community is formed. The sort of community Christians are called to share with one another:

> The way God designed our bodies is a model for understanding our lives together as a church: every part dependent on every other part, the parts we mention and the parts we don't, the parts we see and the parts we don't. If one part hurts, every other part is involved in the hurt, and in the healing. If one part flourishes, every other part enters into the exuberance. 1 Corinthians 12:25–26, *The Message*

Third, Lorna implicitly calls upon faith communities to invest more deeply in the lives of these families. My colleagues and I recently completed a study of how families impacted by disability flourished in a faith community. We learned that while almost three quarters (71 percent) of parents indicated a supportive small group would be helpful to them in raising their children with disabilities, only 11 percent of congregations actually offered such a group.[3] An incredible opportunity exists for the church based on the large distance between these two numbers. While many parents of children with disabilities have been warmly welcomed by the church, others have

3 C. E. Taylor et al, *Welcoming People with Developmental Disabilities and Their Families: A Practical Guide for Congregations*, (Nashville, TN: Vanderbilt Kennedy Center, 2014).

left deeply wounded. When many of these families are able to turn to their congregation in times of need, others have only felt turned away. Supporting the formation and growth of groups like the one Lorna illustrates in this book represents a simple, but powerful, gesture churches ought to make. Since one in four families includes a member with a disability, there is a thriving need right in your midst.

Kathleen Bolduc—author and parent of a son with a disability—describes the hopes of many families, "We trust in our church communities to bear us up during the difficult portions of our journeys . . . we also trust in our communities to share and celebrate the joys of our lives."[4]

This study offers both hope and healing for an often unanticipated journey. Offering a voice of personal experience and a deep love for other parents, Lorna Bradley is an exceptional guide. With this book in hand, there is no need to walk alone.

Erik Carter, PhD

Author of *Including People with Disabilities in Faith Communities:*
A Guide for Service Providers, Families, and Congregations

---

4 K. D. Bolduc, *A Place Called Acceptance: Ministry with Families of Children with Disabilities.* (Louisville, KY: Bridge Resources, 2001).

ACKNOWLEDGMENTS

The journey toward writing this book began years ago by leading a four-week Bible study for parents of children with special needs. When the class ended many parents wanted to continue to meet. As a pastor, how could I say no to that? My search for material written specifically for special needs parents met with little success, and so I spent many years creating my own content for our meetings.

Meeting Kathleen Bolduc formed another important step in my journey. She is one of the early trailblazers writing about special needs family support. Shortly after I launched my first support group, I introduced Kathleen at a conference on the topic of faith and disability. I prepared to lead a brief devotion using the scripture from Mark 10 where Jesus sees the disciples keeping the children away from him and says, "Let the little children come to me." Reading further, the passage also says that Jesus was "indignant." I had an epiphany as I realized how indignant Jesus would be over the way families of children with special needs are often treated. As I finished leading the devotion to those gathered that morning, I looked at Kathleen and said, "We need to talk. I think God just told me to do something entirely different with my life." My doctoral adviser Elaine Heath shared my new vision for providing pastoral care for special needs families and supported me in following my call in ministry.

Scott Basinger, the founding director at the Hope and Healing Institute (HHI) in Houston, came along at just the right point on the next step in my journey. After I was introduced, I briefly described my vision for special needs ministry. He told me my type of project was exactly why the HHI was created. With a mission of "building and restoring lives to health and wholeness," supporting healthy family systems is at the heart of the HHI vision. One month after that serendipitous meeting he handed me the key to my office.

With God's providential timing I met Sue Edison-Swift of Bethesda Institute, who has been an encouraging mentor to me in the final stages of writing. Sue introduced me to Bill Huff at Huff Publishing, and through him, my editor Susan Niemi. Bill and I met in a crowded coffee shop on a cold Minnesota morning, and I knew I had found the perfect home for my book. Susan has been a God-send, and it has been a joy learning from her.

Ultimately this journey began with a little boy who has grown to be a remarkable young man, my son, Craig. He has inspired me, challenged me, strengthened me, and taught me every bit as much as I have taught him. He is my world, along with my husband, Mark, who loves me unconditionally and encourages me at all times. I married well and am blessed beyond measure.

INTRODUCTION

I have hit the bottom of the tank today. We had our annual review at the school, and it's so hard to hear in concrete terms how delayed my son is. I know it. None of this information is new, but it's so hard to hear again. I worry about his future, let alone how we will afford all of his therapies today. Every single day there is so much to do that I feel I can barely keep up. The needs are unending, and I am not nearly enough.

—Blog Post, *Anonymous*

Have you ever been that parent? I have. My experience isn't exactly the same as my friend's recent blog post, but it resonates in many ways. Challenging behaviors at school? Yes! Worry about my son's future? Yes! Endlessly running around to therapy appointments? Yes! A sense at times of being overwhelmed in day-to-day parenting? Yes! A view of the future shaded by anxiety? Yes!

Our journeys as special needs parents are as varied as the differences among our children. Each is unique and precious in the sight of God, and there is no other exactly like our own. Yet there are common challenges and experiences shared among special needs parents. I have led a variety of parenting support groups for more than five years, and it never ceases to amaze me that regardless of how varied the diagnoses within each family, there are common cords that bind us together emotionally and spiritually. Throughout the years I have seen healing of deeply held emotional and spiritual wounds through coming together in a supportive and welcoming Christian community and working through our challenges together.

Through my personal journey as a special needs mom, my experiences as a clergyperson walking with families with special needs, and academic research into how best to build family resilience, I have developed the seven chapters that follow. Each one addresses a common challenge and offers a positive perspective grounded in scripture and practical tools that can be revisited again and again. The chapters are organized to build a firm foundation first by understanding God's character and love for special needs families. Next, there is some heavy lifting involved with exploring deeply held feelings of grief and guilt. Then chapters about patience, self-care, and building healthy relationships offer guidance in strengthening day-to-day resilience. The study culminates in exploring ways that we hold onto hope and experience healing even in situations where there is no cure.

While my original vision for this study involved being part of a small group, I have found that the material also works when used on an individual basis. The Hope and Healing Institute, which supported my post-doctoral research and writing, encouraged me to pilot this material in multiple small group settings in order to fine tune it to be as effective as possible based on survey responses. At times parents would sign up for a small group, but then be unable to attend due to a variety of circumstances. The survey responses from those parents who participated only by reading the material were very positive even without the added component of being part of a community of fellow special needs parents.

If you are using this book as part of a small group experience, there is a helpful appendix beginning on page 103 that includes leader tips, a blessings liturgy, additional resources, and a self-care inventory.

Whether you use this book as part of a small group study or read it on your own, I pray this book provides both insights into a loving God and practical tools for the journey ahead. Encouraging special needs parents is at the heart of my calling in ministry, and I hope that the pages that follow will be a blessing to you.

ONE

I lift up my eyes to the hills—from where will my help come?

My help comes from the Lord, who made heaven and earth.

God and Special Needs

There are a variety of circumstances that set parents on the journey of a life with special needs, perhaps a complicated pregnancy, difficult delivery, medical emergency, illness or accident when a child was young, or maybe a genetic difference. Whether that awareness came at birth or through a process of discovery later on, at some point each of us had a realization that something is unique about our child. Perhaps he or she did not reach milestones at the same rate as other children. Perhaps he or she had unusual behaviors or a pediatrician said, "I would like to run some tests." However the journey begins, soon afterward come the visits to doctors and specialists, seeking diagnosis, direction, and assistance. Life, as anticipated, starts fading from view, and a new and different life takes its place.

A Rose by Any Other Name

Deciding how to refer to people with bodies that function in different ways creates a challenge. There is a varied history of politically correct and not so politically correct descriptions referring to people with special needs. Often times the best way to refer to a group of people is with their own self-definition. However, there is little agreement. What appeals to some is offensive to others. At a recent conference I attended related to theology and disability, some preferred the term "disabled," while others cringed. "Special needs" resonated with some, while others preferred "unique abilities." One person said she liked to apply the term "handicapped" to herself, which received the response, "Really? That would hurt my feelings to be called handicapped." My son refers to what I used to call his "learning differences" as his "learning disability." For those whose bodies function more typically, Dr. Amos Yong introduced me to the concept of being "temporarily able-bodied." Point well made! In whatever capacity our bodies are functioning today, given time they will come to function differently simply due to aging or injury.

For the purpose of this book, a *disability* refers to a way in which a body functions that is not in keeping with its designed purpose. Eyes are designed to see, ears are designed to hear, legs are designed to walk, and brains are designed to process information and social cues, and create appropriate responses. In reality, each person has disabilities, some ability that is lacking either due to illness, injury, aging, or a body that simply never had the capacity to do certain things. I can sing, but I will never do it well because that is just how I was born. I run, but will never break any speed records. It is beyond my ability. I broke my foot in high school, with the result that I can no longer dance on pointe in toe shoes. As I was a dancer at the time, this posed a huge disability! In my everyday life as a person who does not practice ballet, I accommodate the injury and think of it little, though towering stilettos are off the menu. Lacking a physical ability that others have is not a call to judgment. It is reality with which each person copes. As we age, we cope with it more and more. For some, coping with disability requires great effort and daily preparation.

2

In using the term "special needs," I am referring to individuals who need some sort of accommodation in order to help them be successful in their setting. Some are hearing impaired and their special need is for a sign language interpreter or an assisted listening device. Others are visually impaired and may need help navigating the hallways or need access to large-print written materials. Others with cognitive impairment may need lessons to be modified in keeping with their capacity. Still others have behavioral impairment, requiring a modification of the social setting so that individuals do not become over stimulated and anxious. The variety of special needs is virtually unlimited.

Biblical Witness

What is the relationship between faith and disability? There are many passages in the Bible that seemingly indicate a relationship between faith and receiving a cure from a disability. When the hemorrhaging woman touched Jesus' cloak he told her, "Daughter, your faith has made you well" (Mark 5:34).[1] A blind man came to Jesus and he said, "Go; your faith has made you well" (Mark 10:52). After curing the "demon-possessed" boy, a child seemingly with a seizure disorder, Jesus replies to his followers, "For truly I tell you, if you have faith the size of a mustard seed, you will say to this mountain, 'Move from here to there,' and it will move; and nothing will be impossible for you" (Matthew 17:20). There are many more stories such as these that seem to connect faith and receiving a body that functions as designed.

While these miraculous stories are amazing, praiseworthy events that reveal the character of God and the divinity of Christ, these are not normative experiences. Jesus came and cured some, not all. John 5 tells the story of Jesus visiting a pool near the Sheep Gate of Jerusalem. There were five porticos and "in these lay many invalids—blind, lame, and paralyzed" (v. 3). There Jesus healed a man who could not walk and had been waiting at the pool for thirty-eight years. Did Jesus

---

1 All scripture passages are from the New Revised Standard Version of the Bible (NRSV) unless otherwise noted.

heal the rest of people there? We don't know because it wasn't written, but it seems if he had, that part of the story would have been included in one of the gospels. Were the few people we meet in the gospel stories who were cured of physical conditions the only people with faith with whom Jesus came into contact? Surely not! Jesus walked among populations scattered throughout Judea and Samaria and Galilee. Thousands of people traveled great distances to learn from him. Jesus encountered many people with faith. The miracles in which Jesus cured some individuals do not highlight the small handful of people who actually had faith, rather they demonstrate the power of Christ to offer to all an even greater gift, the gift of salvation and freedom from sin and death. How much greater are those gifts than any gift related to our temporary physical bodies?

Faith and Receiving a Cure

Biblical passages about miraculous cures become problematic when they are used as a measuring stick for the level of faith of the parent of a child with special needs. One parent of a boy with multiple disabilities shared that her grandfather-in-law advised her, "If you just dig real deep and pray, God will make [your son] well." She was hurt and offended. "What's wrong with him? He's God's child. This is how God made him, and he is fine." This mother's level of faith was not the cause of her son's circumstance. Rather, her level of faith and understanding of how God sees her son helped her to accept her son as he is, to see beyond his physical differences to the beautiful child of God for whom she will provide care for the rest of her life. In her eyes, the healing that is needed is the world's perception that her son's life is in some way tragic simply because he was born with a body that does not function to the level of expectations of other people.

Is Sin to Blame?

Another theological problem is that some view disabilities as divine judgment for a past sin. This attitude existed well before the time of Christ. In his ministry, Jesus set about changing this misperception.

4

Jesus does not equate disability with sin, as demonstrated in the story of him healing the man who was blind since birth: "As [Jesus] walked along, he saw a man blind from birth. His disciples asked him, 'Rabbi, who sinned, this man or his parents, that he was born blind?' Jesus answered, 'Neither this man nor his parents sinned; he was born blind so that God's works might be revealed in him. We must work the works of him who sent me while it is day; night is coming when no one can work'" (John 9:1-4).

Dr. Jaime Clark-Soles, a leading expert in Johannine literature and professor of New Testament at Perkins School of Theology, provides a fresh perspective on this text. The words "he was born blind" (v. 3) do not appear in any of the early Greek manuscripts. These words were added centuries later. Also early manuscripts had no punctuation. An alternate translation from the earliest Greek texts by Clark-Soles follows: "Neither this man nor his parents sinned. So that God's works might be revealed in him, we must work the works of him who sent me while it is day. Night is coming when no one can work."[2]

The difference in this translation is that the purpose for the man being born blind is not stated to have been caused by God. The man being born blind is simply stated as a fact, and there is no explanation for the reason apart from refuting that sin had anything to do with it.

In Jesus' day people believed that sin caused disability. Little has changed in two thousand years based on stories shared with me by parents who were told that Down syndrome, cerebral palsy, and so forth were marks of God's judgment. The worst example I've heard personally was shared by an adoptive mother of three foster children with severe disabilities. She opens her heart and home and provides care in extreme situations. A person at her church said to her, "If you confess your sins God will quit giving you sick kids." He didn't know her terminally-ill son was a foster child. When he found out weeks later he said, "Well, that explains why you didn't get kids of your own. God sends fit kids to clean mothers. Confess your sins." I think it is pretty clear who is behaving sinfully in this story and who is not.

---

2 Conference session June 2014, access at https://www.youtube.com/watch?v=Z-iUlyLyNtQ

Is sin to blame? Jesus clearly states that sin has nothing to do with disability. Whereas the disciples had in mind the cultural and religious expectation that someone's sin was the cause of the man's blindness, Jesus refutes this idea. Through this man God's glory is revealed. The question remains: Is God's glory revealed only because he was cured? God's glory can be revealed in many ways. You do not have to have a body that works perfectly in order for God's glory to be revealed through you. In this particular story, disability seemingly becomes a potential avenue for God's glory to be revealed to the world. The blindness is not related to sin, but God's glory was revealed through it. Moreover, the glory of God shines through those with special needs whether they are cured or not.

Does this mean God intentionally creates disability, a more-challenging life circumstance, so that God's glory can be revealed? I contend the answer to that question is "no" based on Romans 8:28: "We know that all things work together for good for those who love God, who are called according to his purpose." Not all things are good, but good can come out of all things. It was not good when my father was diagnosed with terminal brain cancer, but there were good things that came out of that experience: moments of spiritual, emotional, and relational healing even in the midst of a circumstance without a cure. As I write this section, I am praying for parents who are saying goodbye to their fifteen-month-old daughter born with Dravet syndrome, a genetic seizure disorder. I pray for God's peace to come to them as they heal from this tremendous loss. What good can come from this situation? That is to be revealed in time. I certainly would not say to these parents in the midst of deep loss, "All things work together for good." That would not be helpful. Yet, in time I know that God can create good out of loss. I have met many parents who, after losing a child, have become trailblazers and guides for other parents, helping them navigate their journey.

Then, Why?

Ultimately, as parents we ask the "why" question. More often than not, the "why" question related to our children remains unanswered. The most common "cause" category for intellectual and developmental disability is "unknown." I do not know why my son is on the autism spectrum. Genetics? Pregnancy complications? Exposure to something toxic to his system? There is nothing and no one to blame, though I tried for a time to assign blame to a variety of sources, including myself. The more important issue to me and my family is seeing how God looks at my child and learning to see him through God's eyes.

As followers of Christ, God does not promise that the road ahead will be smooth and easy. Matthew 8:18–27 provides an example: Jesus is approached by a scribe who vows to follow him wherever he goes. In the very next scene, Jesus and his disciples are out on the Sea of Galilee in the midst of a great storm. The storm, the cross, and persecution all lie ahead on the road of those early followers. Being a Christian comes with no promise of an easy life. Rather, our promise as followers of Christ is that we do not walk that road alone. God is with us, both in the presence of the Holy Spirit and in the people who come into our lives in everyday living and in moments of crisis. God is with us when we gather in a group where we can share the story of our journey and be heard and understood.

God is both for us and with us, and children with special needs stand at the very heart of Jesus' ministry. In Matthew 17, Jesus along with Peter, James, and John, went up a high mountain to pray. While there, Jesus transfigured before them—his divinity shone through his humanity. The disciples experienced the realization that Jesus was the Messiah, with the voice of God announcing the news from heaven to all present. After that mountaintop experience, the very next thing Jesus did was stand with a father whose child had seizures. Not too many chapters later, Jesus rebuked his disciples for keeping children away from him, saying, "Let the little children come to me" (Matthew 19:14).

They Said What?

It is important for parents of children with special needs to have a clear understanding of God and the way that God is with and for them during their journey. At times, well-meaning friends try to offer comforting words that are often not very helpful. In the process they paint God in an unflattering light:

- God must know you are a strong person. God never gives people more than they can bear. *So God decided to increase the workload in your life because you are up to the task? This especially marginalizes the children because the key focus of the journey is about that of the parent, rather than the child coping with special needs.*

- No one can understand the will of God. *So God chose this for you and your child?*

- If you confess your sin and ask God's forgiveness, God will heal your child. *God is vindictive? The circumstance of the child is all about the parent and the child is simply caught up in judgment related to the parent's sin? Again, direct them to John 9:1–4.*

- You shouldn't feel sad. God has blessed you! *Yes, every child is a blessing, but all emotions are valid. There are going to be days when a parent is sad for the harder life their child will live.*

At times it is hard to know what to say, but none of the statements above are helpful. Each of them creates a facet of the character of God that is not in keeping with biblical witness. What can be especially damaging is that a person new to faith may let these not-so-helpful statements form how they understand God, thinking, "Maybe God did do this to my child. My friend thinks so, and she goes to church much more than I do. She must know more about the Bible and God than I do."

The most helpful thing to say to parents of children with special needs is that they are not alone. The character of God is summed up well in 1 John 4:7–21: "God is love." The only reason we have the capacity for love is that "[God] first loved us." Moreover, "there is no fear in love." Starting from an understanding that God loves us as parents and loves our children, work outward from there in looking for how God walks with us on the journey with special needs. It is not only more helpful, but it is much more in keeping with God's character.

Misrepresentations about God's character related to families with special needs reflect our culture in which disability is marginalized. We live in a culture that values money, status, beauty, youth, and high intelligence. It is a daunting list of measures of perfection. Stanley Hauerwas, a theologian, writes, "The most stringent power we have over one another is not physical coercion, but the ability to have the other accept our definition of them."[3] As parents of children with special needs, it is a constant battle to advocate for a child in a culture that pushes them to the margins, defining them as "less than" simply because they are "different than." The differences in our children are often seen as "tragic" by others—and unfairly so.

Where Is God's Heart with Special Needs?

Is this marginalizing attitude in our culture how God sees our lives and our children's lives? Does God see a body that does not function typically as "tragic"? Again, scripture reveals the attitude of God in keeping with God's character. God took on human flesh and came into the world. Also known to us as Emmanuel, literally "God with us," Jesus revealed the purpose of his presence in the world as he began his ministry. In the Gospel of Luke, immediately following his baptism by John in the river Jordan, Jesus returned to his hometown of Nazareth:

> When he came to Nazareth, where he had been brought up, he went to the synagogue on the sabbath day, as was his custom. He stood up to read, and the scroll of the prophet Isaiah was given to him. He unrolled the scroll and found the place where it was written: "The Spirit of the Lord is upon me, because he has anointed me to bring good news to the poor. He has sent me to proclaim release to the captives and recovery of sight to the blind, to let the oppressed go free, to proclaim the year of the Lord's favor." And he rolled up the scroll, gave it back to

3 Stanley Hauerwas, "Community and Diversity: The Tyranny of Normality," in *Critical Reflections on Stanley Hauerwas' Theology of Disability: Disabling Society, Enabling Theology*, ed. John Swinton, 40 (Binghamton, NY: Haworth Press, 2004).

the attendant, and sat down. The eyes of all in the synagogue were fixed on him. Then he began to say to them, "Today this scripture has been fulfilled in your hearing" (Luke 4:16–21).

What is Jesus proclaiming as God's perspective? Jesus, too, lived in a culture that marginalized people with disabilities. Jesus came to proclaim God's will that turns around this power structure. The first become last; the last become first. The oppressed are set free. The year of the Lord's favor, also known as the year of jubilee, was a time when those in power canceled the debts owed to them, and slaves were set free. This practice mentioned in Leviticus 25 began around the sixth century BCE and was celebrated every fifty years. It was a year in which the yoke of poverty was removed and access to opportunity was returned. In declaring the favor of the Lord, Jesus is saying that the ones whom society pushes to the margins are the ones whom Jesus embraces in the center.

Rather than defining people by what they cannot do, we turn the cultural perspective upside down when we look instead at what they can do. A friend of mine has a son whose life is severely impacted by cerebral palsy, "I know there are many things my son cannot do. He will never go to college or get married. But he will also never disrespect me or make choices that break my heart. His life will not be typical, but he has a capacity to love and bring joy. I know he loves me and he is happy." I always feel good when I am with her child. He has a smile that lights up a room and he gives the best hugs. That is a gift.

In addition to bringing to the center those whom society pushes to the margins, Jesus proclaimed servanthood at the heart of his ministry. God humbled Godself and took on human flesh in the form of a man and lived with us, showing us God's intention of how we should treat each other. In the Gospel of John, we read that that Jesus did not display his power on the night of his arrest. Rather, he got up from the Passover meal and began to wash the feet of his disciples in the role of a servant. Parents who have a larger role to fill in raising their child with special needs are likewise modeling the loving servanthood of

Christ by being caregivers of children with extraordinary needs. That does not mean it is an easy role to fill, but neither was the role that Jesus filled.

It is important to note that Jesus did not carry out his journey on his own. He had companions on his journey who supported him and prayed with him. Even at the cross he had some companions who stood by, continuing to provide care even after his death. Women who came with him from Galilee went to the tomb on the third day with ointments and spices. Due to their dedication in caregiving, they were the first to see the glory of the risen Christ. Their servanthood was great and so was their reward. So it goes with parenthood.

There is much to say about God and God's journey with parents raising children with special needs, much more than can be written in a chapter. The main points to take away are these:

- We can trust the Bible in the proclamation that God is love.
- God loves both parent and child, and God is both with us and for us through the entire journey.
- Being grounded in God's love provides firm footing for the journey ahead.

Questions for Small Groups and Personal Reflection

1. In what way do you name the special needs in your family? What names do others use? What is helpful? What is hurtful?

2. How do you feel about the texts in which Jesus cures people? How do you apply them in your life?

3. How has special needs affected your understanding of God's character?

4. How have you experienced the presence of God during your journey with special needs?

5. What are some of your child's gifts and abilities?

Prayer for the Week Ahead

Loving God, we love you and we praise you. We give thanks to you for the children in our lives. Help us and others to see our children as you do. Where some see brokenness of body, you see wholeness and a loving spirit. In Jesus, we see your model of inclusion for all people, and we especially see your love for us. Make us mindful of the ways that you are present with us and for us, especially when we are feeling the weight of challenging days. Just as we are caregivers, bring into our lives those who will care for us on the journey ahead. Amen.

Scripture

I lift up my eyes to the hills—from where will my help come?
My help comes from the Lord, who made heaven and earth.
He will not let your foot be moved; he who keeps you will not slumber.
He who keeps Israel will neither slumber nor sleep.
The Lord is your keeper; the Lord is your shade at your right hand.
The sun shall not strike you by day, nor the moon by night.
The Lord will keep you from all evil; he will keep your life.
The Lord will keep your going out and your coming in from this time on and forevermore. *Psalm 121*

As [Jesus] walked along, he saw a man blind from birth. His disciples asked him, "Rabbi, who sinned, this man or his parents, that he was born blind?" Jesus answered, "Neither this man nor his parents sinned; he was born blind so that God's works might be revealed in him. We must work the works of him who sent me while it is day; night is coming when no one can work." *John 9:1–4*

When he came to Nazareth, where he had been brought up, he went to the synagogue on the sabbath day, as was his custom. He stood up to read, and the scroll of the prophet Isaiah was given to him. He unrolled the scroll and found the place where it was written: "The Spirit of the Lord is upon me, because he has anointed me to bring good news to the poor. He has sent me to proclaim release to the captives and recovery of sight to the blind, to let the oppressed go free, to proclaim the year of the Lord's favor." And he rolled up the scroll, gave it back to the attendant, and sat down. The eyes of all in the synagogue were fixed on him. Then he began to say to them, "Today this scripture has been fulfilled in your hearing." *Luke 4:16–21*

TWO

Blessed are those who mourn,

for they will be comforted.

Matthew 5:4

Understanding Chronic Grief

When my son Craig was young, we were still sorting our way toward a diagnosis for his Asperger syndrome, an autism spectrum disorder (ASD). At the time, he was diagnosed with attention deficit hyperactive disorder (ADHD) and obsessive compulsive disorder (OCD), with additional issues in language processing and fine motor skills. Tourette's and its accompanying tics had yet to raise its head. He struggled in school and in social settings.

Summers were long and difficult with few invitations to play or go on outings with others. Typical childhood activities that break up the long summer months were few and far between. Overnight camps that neighborhood children attended were not for Craig. He could not be successful in that setting. Would the staff be able to handle his meltdowns and temper tantrums? What if there was a fire drill and sensory overload caused him to panic? What if he was bullied, as often happened at school, and with even less supervision? I knew there would be an inevitable phone call asking for me to come and take him home. I did not want to set him up for failure. Church day camps also did not work without accommodations for his needs. In order for him to attend, I had to volunteer the entire time, and my health was not good at the time due to lupus and its accompanying fatigue and joint pain. The regimen of medications I took added to the constant feeling of exhaustion. I needed respite and rest, not more responsibility. One summer I gave in to the encouragement by my pastor to enroll Craig in our church summer camp. The volunteers and staff were not prepared to work with him, and it was clear they resented his participation. I wasn't going to put either one of us through that again!

We finally had a break in the long summers when we were fortunate enough to find Briarwood School, a local school for children with learning differences that offered a summer camp just right for Craig. The director, Vivian Shudde, was passionate about providing camp experiences for every child. Craig could attend four hours a day for two weeks. Camp was long enough to get the socialization he needed, short enough that a meltdown was unlikely; he was home for the evenings so his routine was not too different.

Sometimes Briarwood offered brief seminar topics for parents that were informative and practical. I recall one day when Vivian talked to us about grief. She asked the group if, in the midst of running around for diagnoses, therapies, medications, and meetings, had we ever taken the time to slow down and allow ourselves time to grieve for our children. Her words pushed through my façade, shattering it entirely. I was blindsided by a tidal wave of grief. I started crying. Mind you, not the socially polite kind of crying like heroines in the movies, but that sobbing, entire-box-of-tissue kind of crying.

Embarrassing? Cathartic? Necessary? Yes, yes, yes! I had carried feelings of loss, anxiety, and sadness that simmered under the surface constantly, a cauldron of unnamed emotion. Since it was unnamed, it was also unacknowledged and unprocessed. Was it really all right to admit that I grieved for my child? It sounded selfish. Craig's needs came first, after all. Raising Craig was about Craig, not me. My job was to help him be the best Craig he could be within his capabilities, taking care of his needs, kissing his boo-boos, and being his advocate in a world that he did not understand and that did not seem to understand him. Somehow in the simple offer of giving me permission to grieve, I was blindsided by the reality that I had been grieving for years. I just did not know what to call it. The classic cycles of grief—denial, depression, anger, bargaining, and acceptance—recycled again and again without my understanding the cause nor how to navigate through it.

Is It Really Grief?

In hindsight, it seems odd to me now that I did not recognize the feeling of grief for what it was. Being in my early thirties, I was not well acquainted with the emotion. I had lost three of my grandparents by then and only associated grief with death. I did not understand that grief comes in many forms and is triggered by a variety of losses. Since that time, I have walked with many parents on the journey with special needs and have seen again and again the grateful acknowledgment of naming the unnamed.

The grief felt by parents of children with special needs is unique in a few ways. First, it is often accompanied by guilt. Second, it is chronic in nature, raising its head again and again. Why is guilt attached to grieving for a child? If grieving for a person who has died, or for a lost job, or for the lost companionship of a friend who moved away, people expect to feel that grief. They don't typically feel guilty for grieving those losses because grief would be expected in those situations. Grieving for a child who lives and remains with you daily is an unexpected grief and it goes hand in hand with guilt. One parent shared with me the guilt she felt for grieving for her daughter's Down syndrome. She felt on some level that feeling sad was the same as saying she did not love her daughter fully. Simply by experiencing and acknowledging grief, she felt she was saying that her child was not good enough.

Letting Go of the Expected Child

Why is it not only appropriate to grieve, but normal to do so? All parents have an image of a child that they hope to have one day. That image is filled with hopes and dreams and expectations. There is an expected order to life with developmental milestones leading toward maturity and independence. It is not so much having an expectation of perfection in the child, but rather an image of how that child's life is expected to unfold. Even parents of typically developing children can grieve when their image of a child and their reality of a child do not line up. Often that is a relatively small loss and an easy adjustment. For a parent of a child with special needs, the grief of the loss of the expected child is magnified. It is also normal for parents to grieve things they have lost in their own lives due to a child with special needs. A parent who left his or her career in order to be a full-time caregiver may grieve for the lost job satisfaction, collegial companionship, status, sense of purpose, or even the lost income. Parents may grieve over the knowledge that they will never be grandparents, or that they will never coach their child's soccer team, or any number of life roles that are lost to life with special needs.

No parent hopes that his or her child will have a life of hardship. Of course, every parent expects one's child to face challenges and disappointments. Those come simply by living in the real world. Hardships refer to struggling for even the most basic of skills: physical, intellectual, or social. When learning to walk, and talk, and control body functions and behaviors are hard-fought battles, or entirely unattainable, parents grieve for the hardship that their child endures in a world that expects those abilities. For children trapped inside a body that simply does not work as intended, parents grieve for their child's loss of a typical life and how much harder the child's life may be because of his or her difference. It is normal for parents to feel grief for abilities that are lost in a child's life.

A parent of three typical children once said to me, "I'm not concerned about whether or not my kids are good athletes or good students. Those things are not as important as fitting in socially. Life is very hard for kids who don't fit in." Her words were painful to me, laying bare my son's reality. My grief resurfaced with her words, as well as my private anxiety for my son's future. It was not a grief I felt for myself, but rather a grief I felt for Craig. What would he experience as he grew older? Would he have friends? Would he have a spouse? Would he be able to function well enough socially to hold a job? How could I protect him from feeling the same pain that I felt? To help him with his weak social skills I took him to hours of social skill therapies, learning to make eye contact, take turns, share, and cope with frustration. I did not know, and still do not know, his developmental capabilities. I grieved for how hard it was for him to acquire those skills, one step forward and half a step back.

At the same time that I grieved for Craig's challenging life journey with Asperger syndrome, I appreciated him all the more for his tenacity, for how hard he was willing to work to learn to do what came so naturally for others. That is one of the silver linings that comes with grief, the feeling of joy when those new steps in development do finally come. A father wrote about his son: "The ten years of Walter's life have been ten years of the greatest love and joy imaginable. The love I feel for Walter is so particular to him that it is impossible to imagine that same feeling for a 'normal' Walter. I cannot imagine being as moved by the achievements of a typically developing child as I am with every small step Walter takes in his development. The road is not level for Walter. Every step is uphill."[1]

Why Does Grief Keep Coming Back?

Why does grief for a child with special needs recycle again and again? Grief often becomes especially poignant at times of developmental milestones. First birthdays are supposed to coincide with those first toddling, wobbly steps, except when those steps are delayed by months, or years, or perhaps forever. That is a loss. Every parent yearns to hear "mama" or "dada," but when it never comes, another loss. The reminders of those developmental milestones that are delayed or unattainable

---

1   Richard C. Anderson, "Walter at 10," in *Uncommon Fathers: Reflections on Raising a Child with a Disability*, ed. Donald J. Meyer, 76, (Bethesda, MD: Woodbine House, 1995).

pop up in unexpected places, long after we think we have sorted through grief and loss.

For years we had known that our son's experience after high school would involve a very gradual introduction into a junior college or perhaps a trade school. He needed more time to mature and develop coping mechanisms for the adult world. I knew that clearly and had no other expectations, yet at the time of high school graduation, hearing the various plans of others in his graduating class who were moving away to college, or starting full-time jobs at local stores, or moving into apartments with friends, the reality of Craig's struggle hit home all over again. A few years later I was at dinner with a coworker who was talking about her son who is two years younger than Craig. He was ending his first year of college and making plans for living away from home for the summer as he pursued an internship. I suddenly felt my eyes welling with tears. I was genuinely happy for her son's plans, but was reminded of the pain of my son's fruitless search for a part-time job and the challenges he faced in simply interviewing for a position.

Dana Neider, a parent of a child with special needs and a blogger, writes about the circuitous nature of grief: "Some people navigate through the corridors [of grief] in a pretty direct path (the corridors can lead right in a row: Denial to Anger to Bargaining to Depression to Acceptance). More commonly, you shuffle and wind around . . . leaving the Depression hallway to find yourself somehow back in Anger again."[2]

Grief that cycles again and again can become chronic in nature, and research indicates that chronic grief is common among parents of children with special needs. Feelings of grief need to be acknowledged and addressed. Overcoming grief takes a decision for action. Grief researchers Susan Zonnebelt and Robert De Vries write, "Grief needs an active, intentional decision to face the pain of loss."[3]

---

2 http://niederfamily.blogspot.com/2010/10/amsterdam-international.html?m=1%20

3 Susan J. Zonnebelt-Smeenge and Robert C. De Vries, *Traveling through Grief: Learning to Live Again after the Death of a Loved One*, (Grand Rapids, ME: Baker Books, 2006), 20.

Stages of Grief

Understanding the stages of grief is the first step to getting better control over those roller coaster emotions. In her 1969 landmark book *On Death and Dying,* Elizabeth Kübler-Ross names the classic stages of grief: denial, anger, bargaining, depression, and acceptance. While the grief we experience as parents is different in some ways from the grief of losing someone to a death, the process as it applies to parenting still resonates.

Denial serves as a defense mechanism. It protects us until we are ready to cope. It is those rose-colored glasses that we wear to keep us from seeing what others see. Often denial is broken through by diagnosis, by the blunt words of a stranger, or by the conference with a teacher or other professional who works with children.

Anger empowers, in a way. Once the reality can no longer be denied, anger allows a target of blame for the situation: medical staff, spouse, family, self, child. Anger energizes, but at the same time flares in unexpected ways with, at times, unanticipated targets. Anger may turn inward and become self-blame, guilt, or shame.

Bargaining involves playing "Let's Make a Deal," usually with God, thinking, "If I do this, then you will heal my child." Parents empty themselves, giving all their resources of time, money, or energy for their child. They bargain away their lives or take on the role of Super Parent, in hopes of making a better situation for the child. Parents' needs take a backseat to those of the child. This is beyond typical care giving. It is working under the expectation that the child's disability will be removed entirely if the parent does every single thing that can possibly be done.

Depression creeps in, building like a dense fog, blanketing everything at times. Everyday tasks may become huge burdens; it may be difficult to find pleasure in activities that were previously enjoyable. People may withdraw from contact and isolate themselves. Depression can come out in irritability, inability to function, excessive sleeping or eating, lack of sleeping or eating, substance abuse, retail therapy, or a variety of other symptoms.

Acceptance is the stage when it becomes possible to dream new dreams for the child and celebrate those with joy. An immediate response may be, "Of course I accept my child." Yet, without processing and acknowledging the other parts of the grief journey, acceptance may feel a bit like a dim reflection of reality.

Why Isn't Everyone on the Same Page?

Another issue that comes with grief is that various family members will likely be at different stages. Not everyone in the household will arrive at acceptance at the same time and stay there. Friends and extended family members often dwell in the land of denial for a long period of time. Some never leave it. This can be very painful and has the capacity to cause deep rifts in relationships. I recall when my son was young we were told some difficult results from diagnostic testing. We were dealing with very challenging behaviors at the time and this testing started pointing us toward the autism spectrum. I knew I was getting the right answer to my questions, but it was very painful. I confided with a friend, who then started giving me parenting advice that basically indicated she didn't think it was autism spectrum, rather it was bad parenting on my part. Friends and extended family relationships will be discussed more in depth in another chapter. For now it is worth noting that understanding a friend or family member is in denial may help create more space for understanding and grace when interacting with those people.

Coping with Chronic Grief

What is the path through chronic grief? How do you navigate through it? Primarily, acknowledge the feeling of grief, recognize the significance of what is lost, and then work toward understanding the various facets of the unique journey of raising a child with special needs. Acknowledge that yours is a different experience in parenting, not less, just different.

Emily Perl Kingsley wrote a widely familiar poem, "Welcome to Holland,"[4] about the experience of raising a child with special needs. Kingsley's poem equates the journey with special needs to planning an entire life for a trip to Italy, but arriving instead in Holland and learning to adjust to being in a new and unanticipated destination. She portrays the shock of the unexpected reality of living with special needs and the process of learning to cope and eventually thrive in this alternate place. She writes of the chronic nature of grief felt by parents: "And the pain of that will never, ever, ever, ever go away . . . because the loss of that dream is a very very significant loss."

The nature of chronic grief resurfaces for me with fresh tears each time I read these lines. I shamelessly ask for volunteers to read whenever I discuss the poem in a group setting. There is poignant tension between recognizing the pain that comes with significant loss and the importance of learning to accept the unique beauty in each child. Kingsely continues, "But . . . if you spend your life mourning the fact that you didn't get to Italy, you may never be free to enjoy the very special, the very lovely things . . . about Holland."

Acknowledge your grief again and again as it surfaces. It hurts— that pain demands to be recognized. Handing that grief to God opens a door toward relief from that pain that comes with acceptance.

The Importance of Community

Arriving at acceptance is a journey. One key part of that journey is being part of a community that understands and offers support. Being in connection with other parents who have similar experiences provides relief from isolation and access to shared wisdom. Jesus spoke about the healing power of connection in the Sermon on the Mount:

> When Jesus saw the crowds, he went up the mountain; and after he sat down, his disciples came to him. Then he began to speak, and taught them, saying:

---

4 Emily Perl Kingsley, "Welcome to Holland," 1987, http://our-kids.org/Archives/Holland.html

"Blessed are the poor in spirit, for theirs is the kingdom of heaven.

"Blessed are those who mourn, for they will be comforted.

"Blessed are the meek, for they will inherit the earth.

"Blessed are those who hunger and thirst for righteousness, for they will be filled.

"Blessed are the merciful, for they will receive mercy.

"Blessed are the pure in heart, for they will see God.

"Blessed are the peacemakers, for they will be called children of God.

"Blessed are those who are persecuted for righteousness' sake, for theirs is the kingdom of heaven.

"Blessed are you when people revile you and persecute you and utter all kinds of evil against you falsely on my account. Rejoice and be glad, for your reward is great in heaven, for in the same way they persecuted the prophets who were before you. (Matthew 5:1–12)

We do not have to carry grief alone. We are made for community. We are made to share each other's loads. While grief can be isolating if we allow it to be, we can also choose to find strength through experiencing grief. When we gather in a faith community we can hold each other up and encounter those things that Christ spoke of in the Gospel of Matthew: "Blessed are those who mourn, for they will be comforted." The mourning is hard, but experiencing comfort from God and community in the midst of sorrow is an experience unique to parents of children with special needs. One of the most important and valued gifts in parenting unique children is the people encountered along the way who experience the journey with you.

Carrying the responsibility for providing a level of care that other parents do not experience is challenging. It feels unfair at times, and there are days that are very difficult. Yet, in the midst of that journey we experience the fellowship of carrying each other's burdens, of giving our deepest wounds over to God, and learning to let go. We will always look at the other path, gazing from Holland toward Italy, and think that was my plan too, but we learn new things and have wonderful experiences in Holland that the people in Italy will never know. Jesus offers: "Come to me, all you that are weary and are carrying heavy burdens, and I will give you rest. Take my yoke upon you, and learn from me; for I am gentle and humble in heart, and you will find rest for your souls. For my yoke is easy, and my burden is light" (Matthew 11:28–30).

In Jesus' day, he was referring to the burden felt by Jewish citizens to comply with the letter and spirit of the Torah, Jewish law, but his words and actions in the world also offer relief from other burdens. Let me be clear. In no way am I saying that any child is a burden. Every child is a gift and precious in God's sight. Rather, the responsibility of raising a child whose needs are extraordinary creates an enormous sense of responsibility. The sense of responsibility may weigh heavy at times. Being in Christ, being in fellowship of a caring faith community, distributes the weight of that responsibility across broader shoulders and creates pathways of healing for grief to process and be released.

Questions for Small Groups and Personal Reflection

1. Describe the journey to receiving a diagnosis for your child's special need.

2. How does the word *grief* resonate with your experience?

3. Review the stages of grief: denial, anger, bargaining, depression, and acceptance. Is there a particular stage (or stages) that relates to your experiences? Do you feel stuck in a particular stage?

4. How have you experienced isolation due to special needs?

5. Focus on this scripture verse: "Blessed are those who mourn, for they will be comforted." How have you received comfort when you have felt overwhelmed by grief?

6. What are ways in which you experience hope in the midst of community?

Prayer for the Week Ahead

Loving God, we love you and we praise you. We give thanks to you for the children in our lives. They are a precious gift from you. We pray for them to know your love and presence. We pray for your guidance as parents that we find the right path. We also ask for your comfort. Shoulder with us the responsibility we feel and fill us again with the joy of parenthood. We give to you our grief and ask you to heal it and fill us with a refreshed sense of hope. Amen.

Scripture

When Jesus saw the crowds, he went up the mountain; and after he sat down, his disciples came to him. Then he began to speak, and taught them, saying:
"Blessed are the poor in spirit, for theirs is the kingdom of heaven.
"Blessed are those who mourn, for they will be comforted.
"Blessed are the meek, for they will inherit the earth.
"Blessed are those who hunger and thirst for righteousness, for they will be filled.
"Blessed are the merciful, for they will receive mercy.
"Blessed are the pure in heart, for they will see God.
"Blessed are the peacemakers, for they will be called children of God.

"Blessed are those who are persecuted for righteousness' sake, for theirs is the kingdom of heaven.

"Blessed are you when people revile you and persecute you and utter all kinds of evil against you falsely on my account. Rejoice and be glad, for your reward is great in heaven, for in the same way they persecuted the prophets who were before you. *Matthew 5:1–12*

"Come to me, all you that are weary and are carrying heavy burdens, and I will give you rest. Take my yoke upon you, and learn from me; for I am gentle and humble in heart, and you will find rest for your souls. For my yoke is easy, and my burden is light." *Matthew 11:28–30*

THREE

Wash me thoroughly from my iniquity, and cleanse me from my sin.

For I know my transgressions, and my sin is ever before me.

Psalm 51:2–3

Breaking Free from Guilt

For years guilt would poke me in the side as I slept, waking me up to start the tape recorder in my head. Once again I would be greeted by a familiar list of things I wish I had done differently. Creating a longing for different possibilities, I would roll over and indulge another wakeful night playing the painful game of "what if," a game that nobody wins.

I had a high-risk pregnancy and ended up confined to bed rest for my entire third trimester due to preterm labor. Next I developed pregnancy-induced high blood pressure, which I monitored at home for a week, reporting my readings to the doctor at my next appointment. I was hospitalized and put on medication for blood pressure, in addition to the contraction medication I was already taking. I remember asking the doctor if the blood pressure medication, phenobarbital, would be harmful to Craig. He said it was much less risk for Craig than delivering him at twenty-six weeks due to toxemia. I never asked more questions. Later, as I approached thirty-seven weeks' gestation, my doctor said I could go off of my contraction meds. My husband was going to be out of town that week, so I talked the doctor into letting me stay on my meds one more week since I was still three weeks preterm. I had never made an alternate delivery plan, despite knowing my husband was gone every other week. I wanted him with me when Craig was born and avoided contemplating an alternate possibility. I weighed myself at the doctor's office during that office visit. Usually the nurse weighed me, but I did it that day, distracted and chatty as I moved the weights and balanced the bar. I found out later I did not read the scale correctly. When she weighed me the next week, she noted I had lost five pounds. I had actually lost the weight a week prior when I had weighed myself. I had no clue that weight loss at the end of a pregnancy was so important. When the doctor saw that he scheduled me to be induced the next morning, ironic after months of preterm labor! No inducing was needed because as soon as I went off my labor meds the contractions started. I ended up having an emergency c-section shortly after midnight because Craig was in distress.

So where does the guilt come into play? What if I had known at twenty-six weeks that I should have taken my blood pressure while lying down? It was an awkward process, and I sat up to take readings, causing a blood pressure spike right at the time I was measuring. Why didn't I know that? Did the doctor tell me and I forgot? Did he forget to mention it? Years later I read a study about phenobarbital being linked to a ten-point reduction in IQ and other side effects. What if I had asked more questions about the side effects? I had an excellent doctor who was very compassionate and never left me feeling he was in a rush to get to his next patient. What if I went off my contraction meds at week thirty-seven as my doctor suggested? My husband could have flown home. What if I had not been so helpful and let the nurse do her job adjusting and reading the scale that week? What if? When I see Craig struggle, guilt whispers in my ear, "Maybe things could have been different for Craig. Maybe this is your fault."

Should Have, Shouldn't Have

Guilt is insidious and virtually every special needs parent struggles with it on some level. Birth mothers often carry guilt related to their self-care during pregnancy:

- I shouldn't have worked out so hard while I was pregnant.
- I shouldn't have had that glass of wine (sushi, soft cheese, etc.).
- I shouldn't have gone on that vacation.
- I should have listened to my doctor.
- I should have gone with my instincts.

Guilt is not limited to moms. Parents of both genders can feel guilty about passing on a genetic difference. A father of an adult son with autism told me that he feels guilty over the weight of responsibility placed on his wife as they raised their son, "Somehow I won the lottery, and the most beautiful woman in the world married me. Raising our son has been so hard. I think she would have been better off in a different life, an easier life."

The list of actions and events generating guilt is virtually endless. Parents can feel guilt about an accident or illness that leaves a child with disabilities. Many aspects of a child's therapy: the timing of beginning treatment, the quantity and quality available, and the lack of affordability, may create yet more guilt. Of course therapy generally comes with a regimen of at-home activities, often to be performed multiple times a day. That is just unrealistic in the midst of "real life," but skip a few of those home therapies and the guilt gremlin pops up again. What a child eats or does not eat can cause guilt. If unknown food allergies are discovered . . . more guilt. The enormous amount of time dedicated to a child with special needs may cause guilt because other relationships (spouse, other children, and friends) receive less attention. Let us not forget those "proud moments in parenting" when patience is exhausted. Parents often feel guilty simply for needing a break. It is safe to assume that all parents feel some measure of guilt related to their parenting, but I think it is even more so for parents raising children with special needs. Just as the role of parents of children with special needs comes with a bigger measure of responsibility, so too the accompanying measure of guilt comes as a heaping side order on a plate that is already too full.

The problem with the weight of all the guilt is that, if left to press down continually, it can cause a fundamental shift in self-perception. Hearing how people describe their actions provides good insight into how they carry guilt. A mother of an older teen with an intellectual disability realized after she had tucked her son into bed that she had forgotten to go back in thirty minutes to turn out the light as usual. She noticed the light was still on when she got up during the night. When she checked on her son she found him wide awake at 4:00 a.m., staring at the light overhead. "I felt so horrible. He could have turned out the light, but that's not his routine. He waits for me to come and do it. He had to go to school so tired. I'm such a terrible mother."

This parent's feelings managed to flip from guilt to shame. Shame researcher Brené Brown defines guilt as the realization, "I did something bad." Shame, on the other hand, feels like, "I am bad." Over time we start believing our own negative self-talk. Words matter. What we say about ourselves matters.

A devotion I received used the metaphor of our thoughts forming grooves the way water does as it drips on a rock over time. What kind of groves are your thoughts forming? It is easy to fall into a pattern of negative self-talk that is self-defeating and lowers our sense of worth. Rather than letting guilt pile up, ultimately changing the way we think about ourselves and our parenting capabilities, let's look at some of the foundational reasons underlying our guilt and strategies for addressing guilt head on for a healthier way of coping.

Purpose of Guilt

What is the purpose behind feeling guilty? Guilt is a normal emotion that everyone, apart from psychopaths, experiences at times. Guilt in and of itself is not bad. Psychology teaches that guilt is a social emotion. It stems from living as social beings and sharing interactions with others. People are made for relationship and community. When perceiving that something we have done had a negative impact on those around us, or on ourselves, it is normal to experience guilt. It serves a purpose in motivating a change in behavior. If you feel bad when you do something, you will likely stop doing it. Guilt generally falls into three categories:

- guilt for something you did, intentionally or not
- guilt for something you did not do
- guilt for your situation relative to that of someone else

There are countless ways in which parents of children with special needs can experience guilt in these various categories. I'm sure it is not hard for you to think of several of your own. Fortunately, there are strategies for overcoming guilt.

Reflect on the Reasons for Your Guilt

Is your guilt related to present actions? If related to current, ongoing behavior, what is a strategy that could help you change? A parent shared with me his ongoing struggles to keep his patience while helping his son with Asperger syndrome doing his homework. Just about every day he got very frustrated with his son, and everyday he felt guilty for it. They typically began homework as soon as his son got off the bus because it took him a long time to complete assignments. This father also prepared evening meals and felt stressed to get the homework done in time for dinner. We talked about a way he could restructure their time together after school to avoid frustration. It was a relatively simple solution that worked well, reducing stress for both and breaking the guilt cycle before it even began. When caught in patterns of ongoing behavior that you wish to change, it can be helpful to talk to friends, family, or clergy about strategies for change.

Is your guilt related to actions in the past? One of the gifts of hindsight is the ability to reflect on what we wish we would have done differently. If it is likely that the same circumstances will arise in the future, learn from the past. This blessing can also be a curse. When events of the past have ongoing consequences in the present, coping with that guilt can be a challenge. Parents whose child's disability is related to an accidental injury can struggle greatly with feelings of guilt for not being able to keep their child safe.

While leading group discussions about guilt, I noted a common pattern. Each person could easily offer an example of guilt related to one's child. Also, each person was quick to forgive others, feeling others carried guilt unnecessarily. Yet each parent felt the guilt he or she carried was fully justified, and each one struggled to release it. Each parent was much more willing to relieve another's burden of guilt than to release his or her own, offering grace to others but withholding it from oneself. Sound familiar? It was the same way for me before learning to let go of guilt.

When thinking back on actions of the past, try to remain objective as you would if listening to another person's story. Were your actions appropriate at the time? Were you making the best choices you could at the time given what you knew? Is it reasonable to feel guilty for those actions? A young mother I know feels tremendous guilt for falling down on slippery rocks in a river toward the end of her second trimester, feeling that jolt could be connected to her son's developmental delays. Another mother expressed concern that exercising during pregnancy caused her son's cerebral palsy. In these cases, reassurance from a medical professional could provide some measure of release from guilt. In looking for an explanation for a child's special needs, it is natural to want a source, a cause, a place to lay the blame. Anchoring blame on yourself comes with a heavy price. I know because I did that to myself for years! Acknowledge what is reasonable and let go of what is not. Simply talking to another person about the source of guilt can help a person gain a fresh perspective, process the emotion and related events, and move toward healing.

Finding Forgiveness

Part of healing from guilt involves making amends. When actions causing guilt also cause harm or distress to others, do what is possible to make up for it, whether or not it was intentional. Seeking forgiveness from a person you have wronged can be enormously healing, both in terms of relieving guilt and in restoring the relationship. When my son was in high school, he struggled with social issues and academia in general. During a time of extreme frustration, he asked why he was born with Asperger's. We had talked at times about my being on a bed rest pregnancy, but I had never gone into detail about my sense of guilt and feelings of responsibility for his Asperger syndrome. He was surprised that I would feel that way and was immediately reassuring. "It's not your fault Mom. You did the best you could." Though in my head I knew I had made the best choices I could at the time with the information I had, somehow sharing those feelings with my son finally released me from the guilt I had been carrying. From Craig's point of view, he appreciated hearing more of the story about his birth. Knowing the severity of the complications helped him realize how fortunate he was and reminded him yet again of how deeply loved he is by both of his parents.

Seeking forgiveness is threefold. We need to seek forgiveness from God, from others, and from ourselves. Through forgiveness there is a path to reconciliation and letting go of self-condemnation. In seeking forgiveness from God, the psalmist writes, "Wash me thoroughly from my iniquity, and cleanse me from my sin. For I know my transgressions, and my sin is ever before me" (Psalm 51:2–3). Constantly reliving events through memories and regretful longing for a different outcome perpetually brings guilt to the forefront. Seeking and receiving forgiveness provides release. We can trust in receiving forgiveness from God. The apostle Paul writes, "If we confess our sins, he who is faithful and just will forgive us our sins and cleanse us from all unrighteousness" (1 John 1:9). Simply by asking God's forgiveness, we can trust we will receive it.

In addition to our own reconciliation with God, Jesus taught of the importance of reconciliation with others: "So when you are offering your gift at the altar, if you remember that your brother or sister has something against you, leave your gift there before the altar and go; first be reconciled to your brother or sister, and then come and offer your gift" (Matthew 5:23-34). In Jesus' day, Jews would take a guilt offering to the altar of the temple as part of the process of reconciliation with God. In matters of guilt, the offering was burnt, consumed in its entirety as a gift to God. Other offerings were only partly consumed at the altar, and the remainder was for the livelihood of the priests. In this teaching, Jesus indicates the priority for reconciliation with others by instructing that the guilt offering to God be left waiting in front of the altar until after reconciliation with the person who was hurt by the actions that caused the guilt. The teaching says clearly if your primary offense is toward another person make it right with them directly and then give it over to God entirely.

This lesson is experienced regularly as Christians gather at the table for Holy Communion. In the act of taking Communion, we first confess where we have fallen short and seek forgiveness. In the culminating act of worship, the Holy Spirit is called to be present at the table, making the simple gifts of bread and wine become for us the body and blood of Christ that (in the words of the United Methodist Communion liturgy) we may be, "one with Christ, one with each other, and one in ministry to all the world." The heart of Communion resides in forgiveness and reconciliation with God and with each other.

Sharing Communion with others remains sacred and special to me each time. It is the tangible presence of God's grace in the midst of community. As clergy, there are times when I notice a person who does not come to the table. On one such occasion I got into a conversation after church with a woman who had not come forward. Typically our ushers take Communion to those who remain seated if they have mobility issues. I was concerned that she had been missed. When I said I had noticed she had not to come to the table, she said, "Oh I couldn't! I'm not worthy!" Her statement puzzled me. God calls worthy all who earnestly love God, repent of their sin, and seek to be in union with God. Her tears told me she longed for reconciliation, but the gatekeeper blocking that reconciliation was her own guilt for whatever wrong it was to which she held so tightly. Self-condemnation is a powerful and alienating force.

How do we unlock self-forgiveness? Scripture offers insight: "Little children, let us love, not in word or speech, but in truth and action. And by this we will know that we are from the truth and will reassure our hearts before him whenever our hearts condemn us; for God is greater than our hearts, and he knows everything" (1 John 3:18–19). Our actions indicate how sincere we are in seeking forgiveness. At some point in your life you probably received a half-hearted apology and knew the difference between that and a real one. God knows the depth of our sincerity in repentance for actions that cause our guilt. God knows both our hearts and the reason for guilt that we use for self-condemnation. It is God's desire for us to be released from self-condemnation. God knows all and does not condemn those who repent, those who are truly sorry for mistakes made, whether or not they were intentional. We need to accept that gift and embrace it through our actions. Move beyond guilt by offering forgiveness to yourself. Here are a few activities that may be helpful for embracing self-forgiveness:

1. Talk through your guilt with a trusted friend, family member, counselor, or clergy. Invite into your story those who care about you and are trustworthy.

2. Write a journal about your experience and your journey.

3. Seek forgiveness from others if needed. If it is not possible to seek forgiveness due to death or other circumstances, write a letter of what you would like to say or role-play the conversation with a family member, friend, or counselor.

4. Model showing your love through "truth and action." Being helpful to others moves the focus off yourself.

5. Eliminate negative self-talk that is belittling and damaging to self-esteem. If you catch yourself saying, "I'm a bad parent," follow it with, "That's not true. I'm a good parent. I just made a mistake and nobody is perfect."

6. Do not revisit old guilt feelings. I have long since moved on past my guilt from pregnancy and delivery. When that tape recorder starts again, I hit the stop button, thinking, "I have resolved this and forgiven myself. There is no reason to be thinking about this now. I'm changing the channel."

7. Use scripture to remind yourself that you are worthy of forgiveness to help you release your guilt:

   • "Create in me a clean heart, O God, and put a new and right spirit within me" (Psalm 51:10).

   • "As far as the east is from the west, so far he removes our transgressions from us" (Psalm 103:12).

   • "If we confess our sins, he who is faithful and just will forgive us our sins and cleanse us from all unrighteousness" (1 John 1:9).

These are a few suggestions that may be helpful to you in finding a way to self-forgiveness. I apply them in my own life and find them helpful. One of the joys I have when running is hours at a time alone enjoying the beauty of creation. At times like that when I am free of distractions, I can focus on a piece of scripture and meditate on it in the midst of the rhythm of heartbeats, breaths, and footfalls. On a foggy morning ten-mile run, my running group fragmented across the miles as we settled into separate paces. By the turning point of the final five miles, I was running alone, east into the rising sun, which created spectacular "God light" through the clouds and mist. I focused on Psalm 51:10: "Create in me a clean heart, O God, and put a new and right spirit within me." As the miles passed, a sense of lightness and connection with God filled me, and I carried that centered feeling of inner peace into the rest of the day. I do not even recall whatever guilt it was I was feeling that day, God so fully healed it. Whatever guilt it is that you carry, God is bigger. God forgives, wiping clean the slate for a fresh start. Allow yourself to accept that gift by giving your guilt over to God and taking back a life free of self-condemnation.

Questions for Small Group and Personal Reflection

1. What are some experiences of parenting guilt that you are comfortable sharing with the group?

2. What does guilt feel like to you? Describe using senses or a metaphor.

3. How does guilt impact your life? Do you engage in negative self-talk? If so, how do you plan to change that behavior?

4. What type of guilt are you experiencing? Is it for ongoing issues, or is it for something in the past that cannot be changed? Is something keeping you from releasing your guilt?

5. Describe a time when you offered or received forgiveness. How did it feel to you? How did it impact the relationship?

6. Create a plan for releasing guilt, keeping in mind the need for reconciliation with God, another person, and self. What area needs focus now? What will be an effective strategy for you?

Prayer for the Week Ahead

Loving God, we love you and we praise you. We give thanks to you for the children in our lives. We are sorry for the times when we fall short as parents. Thank you for being with us when we struggle. We trust in your love and guidance and forgiveness. Help us accept those gifts, releasing our guilt for past mistakes and renewing our hope for the future where we will make better choices. We know we will never be perfect parents, but help us be the parents our children need. Amen.

Scripture

Wash me thoroughly from my iniquity, and cleanse me from my sin. For I know my transgressions, and my sin is ever before me. *Psalm 51:2–3*

As far as the east is from the west, so far he removes our transgressions from us. *Psalm 103:12*

If we confess our sins, he who is faithful and just will forgive us our sins and cleanse us from all unrighteousness. *1 John 1:9*

Little children, let us love, not in word or speech, but in truth and action. And by this we will know that we are from the truth and will reassure our hearts before him whenever our hearts condemn us; for God is greater than our hearts, and he knows everything. *1 John 3:18–19*

FOUR

Love is patient; love is kind.

1 Corinthians 13:4

Tools to Increase Patience

Years ago when my son was in elementary school, he participated in weekly group therapy with other boys on the autism spectrum to work on social skills. They were led by a psychologist who worked with them on making eye contact, taking turns, dealing with frustration, and learning social cues. While the kids were gathered with the psychologist, the parents had about fifty minutes, most of which was spent in the waiting room. Waiting rooms were such a big part of my regular schedule then—so many therapies, so much waiting with not quite enough time to leave and run errands, but just enough time that the same magazines week after week were pretty dull. This was before the era of smartphones, tablets, and social media. I led a Bible study the day after group therapy, so I began using my waiting room time to prepare for my lesson the next day. I would sit quietly and read my Bible, taking notes in my leader's guide. But in the back of my mind I had a constant dialogue:

- I hope he is getting along better with the boys than last week. I can't take a meltdown today.
- I hope they get out on time today so we get a jump on the commute home. If it rains again like last week . . .
- How are we going to cram in all of that homework tonight?
- Why didn't I start reading for my lesson sooner? I'm not going to be very well prepared tomorrow.
- I forgot to call the insurance, again. Too late now. It's been on my list all week!

Week after week, it was pretty much the same. As the semester came to an end, one of the other moms said to me, "I just want you to know what a role model you are for me. You come here every week and you are so serene and organized. You've got it together and are so patient. I'm trying to be more like you."

I appreciated the compliment, but I felt like she was describing a stranger. I tried to explain away the façade that she perceived, but she had me pegged to a standard and was happier with her misperception than engaging in an, "I'm just like you!" conversation. I decided to let it go and thanked her, but I really didn't let it go. It stayed with me. How did I look so different on the outside from how I felt on the inside? Where was the disconnect? I doubted I could really be the person she thought I was, but what would it feel like if I were, even for a while? What was missing? Ultimately, the answer that came to me was one word. Patience.

It sounds simple. I will just be more patient. Easier said than done! I needed tools to help the process. A common thread among parents of special needs children is that they have two thoughts about patience: they have more of it than they ever thought possible, and they wish they had even more. It can be challenging to help a child with special needs strive for a new developmental milestone. When helping a child acquire skills that come naturally to others, but remain elusive for him or her, it is easy for frustration levels to rise simply out of an intense desire for the child to succeed in the task he or she is attempting to master. Add on top of that pressures of paid or unpaid work, school, family stresses, and a full schedule, and it is easy to feel anything but patient at times.

Patience Defined

So what is patience? How do you grow it? Most of all, how do you keep from losing it? Dictionary.com defines patience as: 1) the quality of being patient, as the bearing of provocation, annoyance, misfortune, or pain, without complaint, loss of temper, irritation, or the like; 2) an ability or willingness to suppress restlessness or annoyance when confronted with delay: "to have patience with a slow learner"; 3) quiet, steady perseverance; even-tempered care; diligence: "to work with patience."

I find it interesting that this particular definition actually includes a reference to working with someone with special needs.

Wikipedia.com defines patience as: Patience (or forbearing) is the state of endurance under difficult circumstances, which can mean persevering in the face of delay or provocation without acting on annoyance/anger in a negative way; or exhibiting forbearance when under strain, especially when faced with longer-term difficulties. Patience is the level of endurance one can take before negativity.

This definition also resonates well. Special needs parents typically face long-term challenges, and there can be a great deal of physical, emotional, and even spiritual strain. Patience, per this definition, is the capacity to cope positively in the face of long-term challenges and strain. No wonder special needs parents feel they have developed patience due to their experiences with their children.

Patience in the Bible

As Christians, we are meant to strive for patience. It is a virtue to be cultivated. The apostle Paul writes of patience in several of his letters to churches he founded or planned to visit. In his letter to the churches in Corinth, he expounds on the characteristics of love. The first attribute of love is that "love is patient" (1 Corinthians 13:4). Paul writes to the churches in Galatia listing the fruit of the Spirit, the qualities cultivated in your life when living as a follower of Christ filled with the Holy Spirit, "By contrast, the fruit of the Spirit is love, joy, peace, patience, kindness, generosity, faithfulness, gentleness, and self-control. There is no law against such things" (Galatians 5:22–23). To the Colossians he writes, "As God's chosen ones, holy and beloved, clothe yourselves with compassion, kindness, humility, meekness, and patience. Bear with one another and, if anyone has a complaint against another, forgive each other; just as the Lord has forgiven you, so you also must forgive" (Colossians 3:12–13).

Paul writes about patience because members of those churches were divided. In Colossae, the church became divided about heresies, as well as concerns about regulation and ritual taking the place of sincere discipleship. Paul encourages patience in bearing with each other and forgiveness in order to maintain the unity of the church. Similarly, the church in Galatia was divided about circumcision. Some Jewish Christians felt that gentiles must first become circumcised Jews before they could be followers of Christ. The tone of Paul's letter is one of frustration with their inability to solve their dilemma, and so he reminds them that the division they have is not in keeping with the fruit of the Spirit. In Corinth, some members were elevating particular ways of practicing the Christian life as the best way. Some felt having scriptural knowledge and spiritual gifts, such as speaking in tongues, were the best marks of Christianity. Others felt that acts of compassion and mercy were most important, doing all that could be done for the poor, even at great personal cost. These two factions became divided. Paul writes to the church encouraging unity and acceptance of all parts of the body of Christ, including those perceived by the culture as weak, because the body needs all members. People acting out of love toward each other are more tolerant of differences and so he reminds them that "love is patient, love is kind; love is not envious or boastful or arrogant or rude" (1 Corinthians 13:4).

Paul writes of the importance of cultivating patience because even two thousand years ago people struggled with patience. I suppose some comfort comes in knowing it is a universal area for personal growth, but how do we cultivate it? How do we learn to become more patient people, especially in the midst of long-term stress and difficulties? When I think of what it feels like to lose my patience, there comes a tipping point beyond which patience is broken. Per the definition previously mentioned, "Patience is the level of endurance one can take before negativity." Some days the level of endurance is higher than others. Patience comes more easily. Other days, patience evaporates like the morning mist. Learning to identify what triggers the loss of patience can help you to become more resilient, not only in parenting, but in other aspects of life also.

Find the Root Cause

Kathleen Deyer Bolduc wrote a poem "Waiting Rooms" that captures an underlying issue that is part of patience as it relates to special needs. (The entire text is at the end of the chapter on page 56.) In the poem, she describes her emotions as she sits in the waiting room, frustrated by magazines that talk of vacations she will never be able to take because her son would not be able to cope with the stimulation, listening to her son engaging in his sometimes annoying most current repetitive behavior, and sipping tea as she looks at a reproduction of Monet's Garden hanging on the waiting room wall.

I wonder
Can I carve a garden
from the weedy turf of life
plant colors of my choosing
in arrangements pleasing to my eye
weed out thistles
of resentment and fear
replace them with flowers
of joy and contentment?

Resentment is a part of special needs parenting that can be hard to admit. It can help to realize that resentment is not aimed toward the child, but rather toward the condition impacting the child's life. For myself, there are certainly times when I resent life on the autism spectrum. I resent that autism left my son socially isolated as a child and the target of bullying. Living with disability can be highly frustrating, especially in a culture that often marginalizes people with special needs. Diapers for two or three years come with the territory of parenting, but diapers for a lifetime? That's another matter. Maybe you've loaded up the car and driven to a location only to find that the wheelchair cannot be accommodated, and it's the third time this week that has happened. You've planned for months for a special trip only to have illness or behavior cause you to cancel. It is part of the journey for a parent of a child with special needs to look at the lives of other families with typical children and feel resentment for what looks so much easier. Whether fleeting or chronic, resentment is normal.

One parent shared with me that she felt an irrational anger each morning when she dropped off her typical child at preschool. Her son is severely impacted by cerebral palsy and her typical preschool daughter is more than ten years younger. The chronic anger during preschool drop off persisted for weeks. When she dug to the bottom of it, the anger had nothing to do with the preschool or her daughter. She had never before had the parenting experience of an "easy drop-off." She had more than a decade of very complicated drop-offs with wheelchairs and van lifts. That was her normal. She found that her anger was rooted in resenting how easy it was for parents of typical children. Once she acknowledged and processed the feelings of resentment, the daily anger during preschool drop-off disappeared.

When looking at the lot we drew as parents, our lives can look "weedy," as Bolduc describes it. She looks to "weed out thistles of resentment and fear and replace them with flowers of joy and contentment." It can be easy to acknowledge fear of the future, but acknowledging resentment is more challenging. Simply acknowledging having feelings of resentment can trigger guilt. Just as previously discussed in the chapter about grief, unacknowledged resentment cannot be processed. When patience is limited, think below the surface and look for an underlying cause. Is there something you resent? Is there anything you can do about it? Is there someone you trust, a friend, family member, spouse, or pastor, who can listen?

Get a Fresh Perspective

Simply looking at something from a fresh perspective can renew patience. When helping a child strive for a developmental milestone, it may feel as though there is no progress when looking for improvements from day-to-day. Thinking back to the beginning of the journey is a great reminder of how far he or she has come. I recall days when my son was young, and I thought meltdowns were going to be a way of life forever. While I was helping him cope day-to-day, it seemed no amount of therapy and redirection made a difference. However, there was progress. Meltdowns became less intense and then fewer and farther between. These incremental changes slipped by unnoticed. Eventually we reached a point where I could not even recall when the last meltdown had been because it happened so long ago. When Craig faces new challenges, I remind him about how he overcame other adversities in the past, and it encourages him. Looking through childhood photo albums, rereading journals written during a challenging time, and recalling specific turning points can each help you gain a fresh perspective when times feel especially challenging.

Find Your Triggers

There are certain circumstances that create a setting for less patience. While they vary from person to person, common triggers include:

- hunger
- fatigue
- illness
- time
- expectations

Hunger, fatigue, and illness are draining. When small children are hungry, tired, or ill we expect them to be fussy. Our behaviors as adults are not as extreme as those of small children, but there are biological reasons why we have lower reserves of patience when hungry, tired, or ill. In those situations we simply have less energy. When energy is low, patience can be thin. Look for patterns in the times when your patience is low. If you notice you tend to be irritable in the afternoon, what is the root cause? If hungry or if blood sugar is low, eat a snack that is high in protein and complex carbs. This will even out blood sugar and help increase energy levels. Avoid sugary snacks and simple carbohydrates that will send blood sugar on a roller coaster. If tired, take a few minutes to relax. Arrange to go to bed early. If possible, take a nap. There have been times when I used my lunch hour for a quick nap at work, putting my phone on do not disturb and shutting the door and blinds. If you are feeling mentally rather than physically tired, take a break and change your environment. Walk outside for ten minutes and get some fresh air. Unplug from cell phones and social media and enjoy a quiet respite. Alternatively, connect to social media and enjoy virtual community with others. You know what gives you energy. Even small breaks in the day can be highly restorative. If ill, take care of yourself appropriately. Give yourself permission to tell those around you that you do not feel well and you need help so that you can take care of yourself.

Time is a big patience trigger for me. I am probably more concerned about punctuality than I need to be. If I am concerned that I will be late, my patience gets very thin very quickly. I've learned to combat this in three ways. First, I try to build enough time into my schedule so that I do not feel rushed. Avoiding that heightened sense of urgency keeps me calmer. Simply leaving five to ten minutes earlier for my son's therapy appointment makes me much less stressed. Second, I try to avoid over-scheduling. My husband will laugh when he reads this, so I will simply say I put the emphasis on the word *try*. It is not always possible to avoid a busy schedule, but if a day is too full I see what can be rescheduled for another time, or I will intentionally choose a day shortly before or after my busy day and schedule no appointments that day. Finally, when I do feel pressed by time, I stop and ask myself what is the worst thing that will happen if I am late or miss a deadline? Often, the consequences are small. I find I put unnecessary pressure on myself with regard to time. When I take a minute to look at the actual consequences of being late, it relieves my stress and my patience increases.

Expectations cause pressure, which can erode patience. Expectations we place on ourselves can be daunting. It is easy to slip into "super parent" mode where we expect we will always do every therapy exercise assigned for our child, enjoy a career that is satisfying and offers an income that is adequate to the needs of the family, create each family meal with properly balanced nutrition, have an orderly house and yard, and volunteer in our community, church and school. While all admirable goals, reality means that some or all of those goals need to go unmet at times.

Of course the expectations of others add pressure, especially when expectations conflict. A teacher expects your child to complete a homework assignment that strains your child's capacities, and it's the same day as a long anticipated (and rare) birthday party. A supervisor expects a report on her desk first thing the next morning, and you receive a call from the school saying your child is running a fever and needs to go home. Juggling multiple expectations can strain patience to a breaking point, possibly coming out in misdirected ways. Look at the expectations in your life. Are they self-imposed, or do they come from an outside source? Which expectations can be deferred, and which are immediate? Open a dialogue with others who are imposing expectations and look for a solution that is within the capacities of you and your child. As hard as it is to do, ask for help when you need it. I understand the desire to try to handle everything that comes along, but there are times when that is not reasonable. Ask for help. Chances are there are people in your circle of friends who have the spiritual gift of helping and it will be a joy for them to relieve you of some of your stress.

Create a New Routine

If there are patterns to your experiences of frustration, look for ways to change the routine. In the chapter on guilt I told the story of a parent who needed to change his after-school homework routine because he kept ending up in conflict with his child. I was able to suggest to him a solution because I had to solve that same issue for myself and my son. After reaching a point where we both began to dread homework, we created a new after-school routine with decompression time and a healthy snack. We started tackling the most challenging homework first while we were both freshest. Topics at which my husband was the better tutor were saved for later. At times when I felt my patience getting thin I would set a timer for ten minutes and go outside to water some plants, telling my son to keep working and come get me when the timer went off. Essentially, I gave myself a timeout, and that is what I told my son. I wanted him to learn to control his emotions, so I would say, "I am feeling frustrated. I need a timeout." Sometimes he said he needed a timeout too. Well done, Craig! Each of these strategies helped break us out of the homework wars.

Strategies to Grow Resilience in Patience

There are also simple strategies that can be used in any situation in which patience grows thin.

Deep breathing. Neurologist Dr. Andrew Weil recommends breathing in through the nose to the count of four, holding to the count of six, and breathing out through the mouth to the count of eight. Volunteers who breathed this way while being monitored by EEG had noticeably calmer brain patterns.

Breath prayer/mantra. Breath prayer involves picking a word or short phrase and repeating it silently or aloud in conjunction with the pattern of breathing. Breathe in to the thought "Love is patient." Breathe out to the thought "Love is kind." Alternate phrases include: "Breathe on me breath of God," "Create in me a clean heart," or "Let there be peace." Any phrase that is peaceful and centering for you is appropriate.

Exercise. There are physical symptoms that come before a loss of patience: fidgeting, tensed muscles, some describe a tingling sensation. Hard exercise releases pent up tension. Make regular exercise a part of your routine. In the heat of the moment, if appropriate, do some push-ups, crunches, or lunges. Run around the block. Play racket ball against the garage door. At times I would ask my son to run to his room as fast as he could to get something, and I would time him. I would be very impressed by how fast he was and then ask him if he thought he could do it even faster. By the time he raced up and down the stairs five times, he was tired, his frustration was gone, and he was in a great mood from endorphins and playtime. If running in the house is against the rules where you live, a trip to the car in the garage or the mailbox could serve the same purpose.

Journal. Emotions and tension need expression to be processed and released. Some find journaling a great resource for sharing feelings of frustration, resentment, and impatience. Through that process you can gain a deeper understanding of self. If you have concerns about a person reading your journal, use electronic media that can be password protected or secure a written journal in a private place.

Prayer. Never underestimate the power of prayer. It does not have to be a long prayer, and it does not have to be said aloud. Simply pray, "Loving God, I am at the end of my patience. I am overwhelmed and I don't feel I can hold it together right now. I need you to strengthen me. I need you to calm me. I need you to give me peace. Most of all, I need you. Amen." What a powerful lesson for a child who struggles with behavior to hear you pray a prayer like that, or for you to pray together.

Communicate. Talk to someone about your frustration. If a person is the source of your frustration, have a conversation with him or her at a time when you are calm and have a clear perspective. Opening channels of communication is likely to help alleviate the strain. If the source of frustration is not a person, but rather a situation, confide in a spouse, good friend, or pastor who can be objective and help you look for solutions or simply provide a sympathetic ear.

Find support. Being part of a community of people on a journey similar to yours is helpful. It provides a forum where you can be easily understood because others live with situations similar to your own. Find a place where you feel that you belong and can connect in a meaningful way that is rejuvenating. Others with similar experience may have resources and helpful tips that will provide a solution to your problem. Even if others cannot offer a solution, it is healing simply to be heard and understood.

Create a New Attitude

In Psalm 51 the psalmist writes, "Create in me a clean heart, O God, and put a new and right spirit within me" (v. 10). This is a psalm of returning to God and turning away from sin. I think that same idea applies with breaking patterns of impatience, asking God for a clean heart, a fresh start, a new attitude. Think of a time when you have lost your patience and then how you could reframe that in a new way. When I was growing up my father used to struggle with patience. He changed and mellowed over the years. I remember one time driving in the car with him when he was in his sixties, and he missed a green light. As he stopped the car, he turned to me and winked, "Now I'm first! Looking at it that way, it has no control over me. I took its power away." That has always stayed with me. Think of a situation that creates impatience. How can you create a new attitude? How can you take its power away?

Permission to Be Imperfect

Try as we might not to lose patience, it happens. When you lose patience, look at it as a learning opportunity. If appropriate, seek forgiveness of others, including your child. It is good for children to see that parents know how to apologize when they make a mistake. It models that behavior for them. In the United Methodist Church we use the phrase, "We are all going on to perfection. I'm just not there yet."

There are no perfect parents. I think back to my waiting room experience and the other mom who had a skewed perception of me.

I suppose it's nice to think I looked like I had it all together, even if the reality felt far different at the time. Looking back at that time of my life, complete with its "not so proud moments in parenting," I know that I did everything out of a desire to help my child grow into his full potential, whatever that might be. I did not know his capacity for learning, or acquiring social skills, or functioning in the real world without me or his father as a safety net. Ultimately, I think my patience was challenged most by simply wanting the best for my son and being impatient for his future path to be revealed.

The apostle Paul wrote to the churches in Rome, discussing the unseen future. "For in hope we were saved. Now hope that is seen is not hope. For who hopes for what is seen? But if we hope for what we do not see, we wait for it with patience" (Romans 8:24–25). Paul is writing about the hope in salvation that we have, an eternity with Christ in heaven and the revelation of a new creation. It is a hoped for future, but one that remains unseen until the time comes for it to be revealed. As Christians, we live in tension of coping in the presence and longing for a future to be revealed. As parents of children with special needs, that longing for the revelation of a potential future is heightened. What is our child's potential? What does the future hold? In our longing, we rush and expect and frustrate ourselves with our impatience for what cannot yet be revealed. It takes much time. How much easier our path would be if we learn to wait with patience.

Questions for Small Groups and Personal Reflection

1. What are circumstances that challenge your patience?

2. Thinking of Kathleen Bolduc's poem and the line "weeding out thistles of resentment and fear," in what ways have you experienced resentment related to special needs?

3. What experience of losing patience are you comfortable sharing with the group?

4. Looking at the list of triggers (hunger, fatigue, illness, time, expectations), which ones impact you most? Are there others?

5. What are strategies to help you avoid those triggers?

6. Looking at strategies to cultivate patience (deep breathing, breath prayer/mantra, exercise, journaling, praying, communicating, joining a support group), which ones resonate with you? Are there other strategies you can think of? What works for you?

7. What strategy would you like to try?

8. Looking for ways to create a new attitude, how can you take away the power from something that is currently eroding your patience?

Prayer for the Week Ahead

Patient God, we read in the Psalms about how you are slow to anger and patient with us when we fall short. We are made in your image. Help us, too, to be slow to anger. We trust in you as our guide and the quiet center when we feel overwhelmed. We pray for your peace that surpasses all understanding to come and fill us. Help us to grow in patience and be the people you call us to be. Amen.

Scripture

For in hope we were saved. Now hope that is seen is not hope. For who hopes for what is seen? But if we hope for what we do not see, we wait for it with patience. *Romans 8:24–25*

By contrast, the fruit of the Spirit is love, joy, peace, patience, kindness, generosity, faithfulness, gentleness, and self-control. There is no law against such things. *Galatians 5:22–23*

As God's chosen ones, holy and beloved, clothe yourselves with compassion, kindness, humility, meekness, and patience. Bear with one another and, if anyone has a complaint against another, forgive each other; just as the Lord has forgiven you, so you also must forgive. *Colossians 3:12–13*

Love is patient; love is kind; love is not envious or boastful or arrogant or rude. It does not insist on its own way; it is not irritable or resentful; it does not rejoice in wrongdoing, but rejoices in the truth. It bears all things, believes all things, hopes all things, endures all things. Love never ends. But as for prophecies, they will come to an end; as for tongues, they will cease; as for knowledge, it will come to an end. For we know only in part, and we prophesy only in part; but when the complete comes, the partial will come to an end. When I was a child, I spoke like a child, I thought like a child, I reasoned like a child; when I became an adult, I put an end to childish ways. For now we see in a mirror, dimly, but then we will see face to face. Now I know only in part; then I will know fully, even as I have been fully known. And now faith, hope, and love abide, these three; and the greatest of these is love. *1 Corinthians 13:4–13*

Waiting Rooms

by Kathleen Deyer Bolduc

I spend so many hours
in waiting rooms
pediatrician, neurologist
behavioral specialist, psychiatrist
school psychologist, play therapist
so many doctors
so much advice
so little understanding
What do they know
(despite diplomas
on sterile walls)
of living with disability?

It's different here
This therapist knows disability
It moved in some twenty-some
    years ago
with her firstborn child
She plays with my son
leaving me alone
with a cup of tea, my thoughts, and
    magazines

Travel & Leisure, Smithsonian,
    Family Fun
Sometimes I read them and fume
What happened to my family's fun?
Only the beach for us
familiar and undemanding
No museums or theme parks
too stimulating
No long road trips stopping
at motels with pools each night
too disruptive

Above the magazine rack
brochures offer a better life
Women's Mind-Body Wellness,
Natural Wellness & Healing
Conflict Management
I hear my son's laughter
The sound of knocking on flimsy
    walls
his current game, sometimes funny
sometimes enough to make me
    scream stop

I sip raspberry tea
and step into Monet's garden
onto a bridge awash
in a dream of green
countless scenes of beauty
just outside the cottage door
waiting for the artist's brush

I wonder
Can I carve a garden
From the weedy turf of life
plant colors of my choosing
in arrangements pleasing to my eye
weed out thistles
of resentment and fear
replace them with flowers
of joy and contentment?

Suspended between past and future
in this waiting room
today
I weave a garden plan of beauty
while I wait
for my son

FIVE

He said to them, "Come away to a deserted place all by yourselves and rest a while."

For many were coming and going and they had no leisure even to eat.

And they went away in a boat to a deserted place by themselves.

Mark 6:31–32

Self-care for Caregivers

I recently attended a retreat for clergy of the United Methodist Church. We gathered at a rustic retreat facility deep behind the piney curtain of east Texas enjoying the opportunity to disconnect from the pace of ministry and reconnect with each other in a sacred space. We participated in a variety of workshops that encouraged personal reflection. One workshop leader, Cindy Serio of MOSAIC Spiritual Formation Ministry, had us sit quietly and practice a deep-breathing exercise. We began breathing at the rhythm that she dictated. Breathing in and holding, breathing out and holding. She led us into longer and deeper breaths with longer periods of time in between. At first the exercise was soothing, but as the pauses between breaths got longer and longer, I began to grow uncomfortable. As a runner, I have pretty good lung capacity, but I could not exhale and keep my lungs empty for as long as she required. My oxygen-starved body grew very uncomfortable. I started seeing dots and my lungs burned. This was a relaxation exercise?

Try as I might, I had to have air. I chalked it up to a recent bout of the flu and pneumonia. I cheated and inhaled just a little. Who would know? Then I had to do it again. I marveled at Cindy's lung capacity and felt like a failure when we finished the activity. Afterwards, Cindy asked who had to breathe. Every hand went up. "Good. You each showed compassion to yourself. It is hard to offer compassion to others when you won't offer it to yourself."

Self-care As Self-compassion

Clergy are wired to offer compassion to others, putting the needs of others first and serving as needed. In many ways, I find parallels between clergy and parents of children with special needs. In both callings there is a whole lot of giving and whole lot of putting your own needs behind those of others, particularly when the needs of others are critical. Another parallel I see is that clergy are notoriously bad at self-care, as are special needs parents. There must be a balance between giving to others and caring for self. Often the balance tips too much toward doing for others at the cost of exhaustion and burnout. This can lead to compassion fatigue, a situation in which it becomes increasingly difficult to offer compassion to others at the level previously available.

Constantly giving without taking time to recharge your own batteries comes at a price. I noted in the breathing exercise that when my lungs were full, I could hold my breath a long time before I felt uncomfortable. I had a reserve of air that easily sustained me while holding my breath. However, when I held my breath with my lungs empty, I became distressed quickly. There was no reserve and my ability to cope with the exercise was greatly limited when I was empty.

Lesson learned. I cannot run on empty. Neither can you.

When our reserves are full, it is much easier to cope as special needs parents with the unexpected call from school, the medical crisis, the rounds of therapy, the meltdowns, and so forth. Even as we offer care to our children and support them in ways that may feel extraordinary, so too do we need to offer care to ourselves. Our batteries need to be recharged on multiple levels: physically, emotionally, and spiritually. John Swinton, a noted author in the field of theology and disability, spoke at a conference that I attended in Houston, saying, "Diagnoses have biological, social, and spiritual implications." The reality Swinton stated applies to each member of the family: child, parent, and siblings. Therefore, it is critical to provide self-care in each of those areas to keep ourselves functioning well.

Jesus and Self-care

As Christians some may feel they are called to give selflessly and endlessly, but the Bible models for us self-care even in the midst of caring for others. In Matthew 14, John the Baptist was beheaded by King Herod. The story continues: "Now when Jesus heard this, he withdrew from there in a boat to a deserted place by himself. But when the crowds heard it, they followed him on foot from the towns. When he went ashore, he saw a great crowd; and he had compassion for them and cured their sick" (Matthew 14:13–14).

Jesus tried to set aside time for himself, perhaps to mourn the death of his cousin, perhaps to move farther from the reach of Herod, perhaps to avoid crowds drawing Herod's attention to his ministry. But the people heard where he was going, and they raced there ahead of him. His search for respite turned into an opportunity for compassion and healing. When the evening came there was no food. His disciples urged him to send the crowds away so they could get food in the local villages. Instead, Jesus multiplied the five loaves of bread and the two fish and fed them all.

So where does the self-care come in? Isn't this an example of self-care gone wrong with life interrupting and taking away the chance for respite? Here is the rest of the story: "Immediately he made the disciples get into the boat and go on ahead to the other side, while he dismissed the crowds. And after he had dismissed the crowds, he went up the mountain by himself to pray" (Matthew 14:22–23). Though Jesus' plan for respite was interrupted, by the end of the day he made time for it. He took care of the pressing needs of the crowd and the disciples and then sent them all away so that he could be alone. Was this to recharge spiritually? Did he rest while alone to recharge physically? Did he grieve for John during his time of prayer, processing emotions of loss? Perhaps he did all three. What we do know is that Jesus made self-care a priority, even in the midst of tremendous pressure. It may be easy to think the needs of our family are just too much for us to take a break, but could the needs of our family really compare to the needs and expectations laid on Jesus?

If anyone had an excuse to ignore self-care, it would be Jesus, with the weight of the world on his shoulders in the form of the cross to come. Yet, time and again Jesus models healthy self-care.

He said to them, "Come away to a deserted place all by yourselves and rest a while." For many were coming and going, and they had no leisure even to eat. And they went away in the boat to a deserted place by themselves (Mark 6:31–32).

When Jesus realized that they were about to come and take him by force to make him king, he withdrew again to the mountain by himself (John 6:15).

But now more than ever the word about Jesus spread abroad; many crowds would gather to hear him and to be cured of their diseases. But he would withdraw to deserted places and pray (Luke 5:15–16).

In the morning, while it was still very dark, he got up and went out to a deserted place, and there he prayed (Mark 1:35).

After saying farewell to them, he went up on the mountain to pray (Mark 6:46).

Now during those days he went out to the mountain to pray; and he spent the night in prayer to God (Luke 6:12).

At that time Jesus went through the grainfields on the sabbath; his disciples were hungry, and they began to pluck heads of grain and to eat (Matthew 12:1).

One day he got into a boat with his disciples, and he said to them, "Let us go across to the other side of the lake." So they put out, and while they were sailing he fell asleep (Luke 8:22–23).

In these passages, Jesus models good self-care. He takes care of his spiritual life through prayer. There are additional passages referencing his practice of fasting, reading scripture, and engaging in community. He cares for himself physically through sleeping and eating, even when circumstances or customs dictate that he should not do so. He and his followers are frequently criticized for the company they keep at the dinner table, what they eat, and when they eat it. Jesus also takes care of himself emotionally by periodically withdrawing from guiding and caring for others. There are many stories of the crowds pressing in on him, following him, racing ahead to where they expect he will be. He periodically withdraws from that intense pressure, setting aside for a while the needs and expectations of others. Additionally, the Bible recounts Jesus' healthy expressions of anger, grief, and other emotions, which are part of emotional self-care. I especially enjoy the story of the crowd coming to "take him by force" and make him king. Have you ever had folks volunteer you to do something that you didn't want to do? Jesus even models for us that it is okay to say, "No."

Family Impact of Self-care

It is important to understand the value of self-care and its positive impact on family. I recall when preflight instructions on airplanes changed to include the line about persons traveling with small children should put on their own air mask first. At first it sounded selfish, but after I thought a bit it made a lot of sense. By doing it in that order, everyone survives. Likewise, when parents engage in good self-care, the family as a whole grows more resilient. This is a critical point. The divorce rate in special needs families is much higher than in families with typical children. Finding relief from stress and engaging in good self-care raises resilience for the entire family.

Children are in tune to the emotions around them. When my spouse or son comes home after a bad day, I can pick up on his mood as he walks through the door. The furrowed brow, drooped shoulders, and clenched jaw tell the story. The words that follow merely fill in the details. Parents who are chronically anxious, depressed, physically exhausted, and stressed convey those feelings to the rest of the family. Conversely, parents who are rested, relaxed, content, and resilient resonate that energy into the home as well. Everyone has good days and bad days. That is simply part of life. No parent will be "happy, perky" all the time. That is an unreasonable expectation. However, engaging in healthy self-care provides the needed reserve for dealing with bad days by providing physical, emotional, and spiritual reserves.

Impediments to Self-care

What gets in the way of self-care? Many things, but the biggest offenders are time, opportunity, guilt, and priorities. Parenting is a big job, made even bigger by parenting a child whose needs are great. It feels at times as though twenty-four hours in a day simply aren't enough. Often the only time parents have to themselves is when their children are at school or when they have a lunch break at work. It takes creativity to find more time and make good use of the free time you do have. Simply finding the opportunity for self-care creates its own challenges. Sometimes participating in the self-care we would most like to do involves coordinating challenging schedules and engaging resources (child care, finances, travel, etc.) that seem all but impossible to bring together.

I discussed the role of guilt in a previous chapter. Relative to self-care, guilt has a negative voice that says, "I shouldn't need a break. I don't need help. I know I ought to go see a doctor about . . . but . . ." That voice cannot be the one that wins. Finally, making self-care a priority is its own challenge. Most folks accept the value of self-care. We like the idea of it. Actually engaging in self-care takes changing the mindset from valuing the idea of self-care to embracing self-care as critically important for physical, emotional, and spiritual health. In the moment, things that seem urgent can get in the way of self-care.

Urgent Versus Important

Back in 1967 Charles Hummel wrote *Tyranny of the Urgent* on the topic of how urgent interruptions in lives take the focus away from what is important. Hummel offered a good model for time management from a Christian perspective. His writing centered on learning to lead a God-centered life and taking control of how we use time in order to make that a priority. His four-point approach applies universally for setting and keeping priorities:

- Decide what is important.
- Evaluate how time is used.
- Set priorities by budgeting time.
- Follow through.

Again, we can find in the Bible that Jesus models how to overcome obstacles of time, opportunity, and priorities. Think of how Jesus used his time. He did many things, but after three years of ministry, on the night of his arrest he said, "I glorified you on earth by finishing the work that you gave me to do" (John 17:4). What had he finished? Had he done every possible thing? Had he cured every person? Had he thrown Rome out of power in Jerusalem, releasing people from oppressive authority? Had he fulfilled the expectations of all people, including those who wanted to take him by force and make him king?

The needs of the people were many and urgent, but his focus was on what was important. In the midst of ministry he took time away for solitude, prayer, fasting, and worshiping in community. He built relationships, taking time to listen to people, talking to them and teaching. As he cut through Samaria with his disciples on his way from Jerusalem to Galilee, he stopped by a well and spoke with a woman there in the hot afternoon sun and then delayed his departure by days to spend extra time in Samaria. His life was busy. Yes. But out of control? No. Why? This story shows us:

> Now as they went on their way, he entered a certain village, where a woman named Martha welcomed him into her home. She had a sister named Mary, who sat at the Lord's feet and listened to what he was saying. But Martha was distracted by her many tasks; so she came to him and asked, "Lord, do you not care that my sister has left me to do all the work by myself? Tell her then to help me." But the Lord answered her, "Martha, Martha, you are worried and distracted by many things; there is need of only one thing. Mary has chosen the better part, which will not be taken away from her" (Luke 10:38–42).

Martha attended to what was urgent. Mary attended to what was important. I've been Martha, busy and distracted and resentful of others who do not share my burden. I've been Mary at times, too, letting go of the guilt of not doing everything and appreciating the gift of taking time to attend to what is important, including doing something for myself when I need a break. There will always be more to do than can possibly be done, and the opportunity to be busy is always present.

Engaging in Self-care

Now that we have a better understanding of why self-care is important, how do we begin to shift priorities to make time for it? What are some practical tips for better self-care that fit into a special needs parent's lifestyle? There are many options, and the goal here is not to cause anyone to feel guilty for what they ought to be doing. Rather, look for self-care ideas that resonate with you and think of what you would like to try to do. There are physical, emotional, and spiritual self-care inventories for you to complete on pages 117–119. These tools provide a way to identify quickly how to improve your self-care in ways that are most meaningful to you.

Physical Self-care

Get adequate sleep. Taking a brief nap or even lying down for a while is surprisingly helpful. Be proactive in meeting your need for rest. My spouse and I both worked full-time when our son was young. We each got one sleep-in day on the weekend, knowing the other would get up with our son that day. I often have insomnia in the middle of the night. I've found listening to a podcast "talks" me to sleep in about ten minutes. A friend of mine uses those wee hours of wakefulness for prayer.

Eat a balanced diet. There is plenty of easily accessible information about diet. Eating well translates into feeling well and having a higher level of energy. Attempting a radical and drastic diet-makeover is overwhelming for most people. Start by making just one change, such as keeping healthy snack items in your house or car or trying a healthy food that is new to you. Keeping a food journal can help pinpoint areas for improvement.

Drink plenty of water. Keep a refillable container on hand at work, in the car, and near your favorite chair at home. If it is handy you are more likely to drink it.

Exercise. Moderate physical activity reduces stress, releases toxins, elevates mood, improves cardiovascular health, and reduces risk for a variety of medical conditions such as high blood pressure, cancer, and stroke. Even simple activities like going for a walk regularly or practicing yoga briefly each day can be very beneficial.

Relax. Enjoy the peace that comes with simply being still. Release tension in tight muscles through stretching, a hot bath, or massage. Like many other folks, I tend to hold tension in my neck and shoulders. I keep a foam roller handy for quick and easy self-massage to avoid headaches and reduce tension.

Get an annual flu shot. Avoiding the flu is better for the entire family, especially if you are raising a child with a weak immune system. Check with your family doctor first. Some children cannot be exposed directly to the vaccine or to people who have recently been vaccinated.

See a doctor as needed. Get an annual physical and keep current on tests such as cholesterol screening, mammograms, bone density,

PSA, and so forth. If you are experiencing symptoms, do not ignore them. Granted, this is not the most fun and exciting part of self-care, but it is important for well-being.

Avoid overconsumption of alcohol, as well as tobacco and other addictive agents. Addictions have an enormously negative impact on physical health. If you think you have a problem, seek appropriate assistance.

Emotional Self-care

Be mindful of your emotions. Especially notice emotions that dominate in ways that have a negative impact on you or your family: anger, depression, anxiety. Look for underlying causes when stuck in particular emotions. Accept all emotions as valid. Allow yourself to feel what you feel.

Nurture friendships. It is important to have close friends who are trustworthy and can help process life experiences that are challenging, as well as celebrate joys.

Spend time in prayer. Talking with God is like talking with your closest friend who knows you better than you know yourself. Emotional healing and emotional health happen through prayer.

Enjoy time with your child. Spend time just having fun with your child without a goal for development or therapy. Simply have fun together.

Schedule family time. Families that spend time together have a higher level of resilience and their children are overall more successful regardless of their developmental capacity.

Pay attention to self-talk. Is your self-talk positive (Yes I can! I tried my best) or negative (Why do I bother? My family would be better off without me). Reshaping self-talk positively is a powerful tool in emotional health. Refute negative self-talk with, "That's not true . . ."

Set aside time for yourself. Take a break and relax when you can. Regularly do something you enjoy whether it's going outside, reading, or meeting a friend. Make it a priority to do what makes you happy at least for a little while each day.

Find ways to reduce stress. Do not take on more than you can handle. It is okay to say, "No." It is also okay to say, "Yes." (Do you need a break? Would you like some help? How about a night out?)

Engage in your favorite hobbies. Take time to enjoy the things that most inspire you, help you relax, or create contentment.

Practice gratitude. Every day say aloud something you are grateful for. Make it part of the family meal, with everyone sharing their thankfulness. Write them on a list and add to it every day.

Keep a journal. Journaling can be highly effective in processing emotions.

Join a support group. It is helpful to join with others who share your experiences, allowing you to talk openly and be heard.

Talk to a counselor. A trained professional is a valuable asset for emotional health. Check with your insurance plan for counselors who are in network. Clergy can often recommend good counselors.

Spiritual Self-care

Spiritual self-care is intentional focus of time and energy on your relationship with God. Richard Foster, author of *Celebration of Discipline* and a leading expert on spiritual self-care, offers the following suggestions as ways you can enrich your spiritual life.

Internal disciplines. These disciplines focus on your spiritual life through internal reflection.

- Pray—talk with God as a friend.
- Meditate—focus on a word or one aspect of God in your life.
- Study scripture—read a verse at a time or a larger text.
- Journal—write thoughts about your spiritual life.
- Be silent/listen—find quiet space to focus on God's message to you.
- Fast—take a fast not only from food, but from distractions such as television.

Outward disciplines. These disciplines are expressed in personal actions and outward manifestations.

- Solitude—set aside time to be apart from others to focus on God.

- Simplicity—embrace a practice of "enough" and let go of wanting more.

- Submission—follow where God leads.

Corporate disciplines. These disciplines are experienced with others.

- Worship—participate regularly in worship, including the sacraments.

- Service—serve as God's hands and feet in the world in help to others.

- Community—engage as part of a Christian community where you can share your talents with others, as well as be supported.

Each of these lists for self-care offers good starting points. There are many additional options. The checklist tool on page 117 is to help you assess your self-care in all three areas: physical, emotional, and spiritual. There are some blank lines for you to add your own ideas. Read the list and mark what you already do as well as your level of interest in trying new activities in self-care. Celebrate the ones that you already do. Well done! Look for what interests you as something you would like to add as self-care and make an intentional plan to try it. Be specific about what you will do, when you will do it, and for how long. Write it down and post it someplace as a reminder. Here are some examples:

- I will take a twenty-minute walk on Monday, Wednesday, and Friday after dropping the kids at school or after work (physical and emotional self-care).

- I will set a lunch date with a good friend this week (emotional self-care).
- I will get a flu shot the next time I pick up a prescription (physical self-care).
- I will subscribe to a daily Bible reading plan (spiritual self-care).
- I will meditate for ten minutes before I go to bed (emotional and spiritual self-care).
- I will schedule my annual physical and screening tests (physical self-care).
- I will meet a friend at the gym twice this week (physical and emotional self-care).
- I will sign up for the adult soccer team at work (physical and emotional self-care).

A mother who participated in one of my pilot groups when this book was under development offered the following powerful story and has given permission to share it in hopes that it makes a difference for even one person:

My son is twelve years old and has Asperger syndrome. He is very high functioning. Even so, he depends on me daily for many things.

The day after his tenth birthday party, the doctor called to tell me I had breast cancer. After I got the call from the doctor, I cried and then I prayed to God to let me live for my son's sake. I was forty-five. I was lucky; they'd caught it early. The cancer was stage 1A and only 5 mm or 1/6th of an inch. My cancer was treated, and I am cured.

You've heard early detection saves lives. What early detection did for me was to allow me to be with my son almost as much as normal. It allowed me to choose lumpectomy over mastectomy. That choice meant hours in the hospital, not days—and only weeks recovering, not months. Caught early, the cancer hadn't spread outside the breast. So I had only six weeks of radiation, five days a week, for fifteen minutes, while my son was in school. I didn't have to endure months of hours-long chemotherapy treatments and its side effects.

Illness can strike anybody at any time. But for those of us with special needs children, such illness can have a much greater impact on the children that depend so much on us. I wanted to share my story and echo Lorna's recommendation to "See a doctor as needed. Get an annual physical and keep current on tests."

Even with early detection, sometimes a cure is not always possible, as was the case with my father. Nevertheless, his early diagnosis was still a gift in that it allowed time for us to process as a family what was coming in the not too distant future. He was able to make the most of every day and set priorities for his remaining time.

Whatever you choose as self-care, you may need to be creative to make it happen. Years ago I was floundering for a lack of self-care. As Mother's Day approached my husband asked what I wanted, and I told him I wanted time to read a book. In my mind, it was an impossible gift, and I'm sure I had a less than kind tone of voice when I said it. Not one of my finer moments! That memory is a good reminder about how lack of self-care has a negative impact on the rest of the family. On Mother's Day he gave to me a gift card to a bookstore and another to a coffee shop. He told me to take a break when I needed one, and he would cover at home. With the dollar amount at the coffee shop, he probably envisioned me having a large blended beverage and a pastry on every trip. I had the small house coffee and stretched that card out for months! When I felt self-care was impossible and was resentful about it, my spouse helped me come up with a plan to get the break I needed. In the process, the whole family was blessed by my improved mood and energy level. Self-care is not an indulgence. It's a necessity for maintaining all around health and resilience.

Questions for Small Groups and Personal Reflection

Have available extra copies of the self-care inventories from pages 117–119 for those who may be sharing a book or may not have their book with them.

1. Review your completed checklist or take a few minutes to complete it now.

   • How do you feel about the importance of self-care?

   • What gets in the way of doing good self-care?

   • How can you make space for self-care?

   • Do you need to stop or modify something in your life in order to engage in better self-care?

2. Create an intentional action plan.

   • Looking at physical self-care, what do you already do? What would you like to try? Any additional suggestions?

   • Looking at emotional self-care, what do you already do? What would you like to try? Any additional suggestions?

   • Looking at spiritual self-care, what do you already do? What would you like to try? Any additional suggestions?

   • What is your intentional action plan for self-care? Write down what you will do, when you will do it, and for how long.

Prayer for the Week Ahead

Caring God, we thank you for the way you care for us, sometimes in unseen ways. We trust in Christ and the ways he modeled self-care for us. Yet, at times we let the world and responsibilities keep us from caring for ourselves. Help us to practice your choices of how we should care for our bodies, minds and souls. Amen.

Scripture

Now as they went on their way, he entered a certain village, where a woman named Martha welcomed him into her home. She had a sister named Mary, who sat at the Lord's feet and listened to what he was saying. But Martha was distracted by her many tasks; so she came to him and asked, "Lord, do you not care that my sister has left me to do all the work by myself? Tell her then to help me." But the Lord answered her, "Martha, Martha, you are worried and distracted by many things; there is need of only one thing. Mary has chosen the better part, which will not be taken away from her." *Luke 10:38–42*

Now when Jesus heard this, he withdrew from there in a boat to a deserted place by himself. But when the crowds heard it, they followed him on foot from the towns. When he went ashore, he saw a great crowd; and he had compassion for them and cured their sick. *Matthew 14:13–14*

He said to them, "Come away to a deserted place all by yourselves and rest a while." For many were coming and going, and they had no leisure even to eat. And they went away in the boat to a deserted place by themselves. *Mark 6:31–32*

When Jesus realized that they were about to come and take him by force to make him king, he withdrew again to the mountain by himself. *John 6:15*

But now more than ever the word about Jesus spread abroad; many crowds would gather to hear him and to be cured of their diseases. But he would withdraw to deserted places and pray. *Luke 5:15–16*

In the morning, while it was still very dark, he got up and went out to a deserted place, and there he prayed. *Mark 1:35*

After saying farewell to them, he went up on the mountain to pray. *Mark 6:46*

Now during those days he went out to the mountain to pray; and he spent the night in prayer to God. *Luke 6:12*

At that time Jesus went through the grainfields on the sabbath; his disciples were hungry, and they began to pluck heads of grain and to eat. *Matthew 12:1*

One day he got into a boat with his disciples, and he said to them, "Let us go across to the other side of the lake." So they put out, and while they were sailing he fell asleep. *Luke 8:22-23*

SIX

But Ruth replied, "Don't ask me to leave you and turn back.
Wherever you go, I will go; wherever you live, I will live.
Your people will be my people, and your God will be my God.

Ruth 1:16 *NLT*

Building Healthy Relationships

I recall when my son was a newborn we were both absolutely fascinated with each other during our "honeymoon phase," constantly looking at each other and studying every tiny detail. Once he was a little older, I loved to make faces and watch his reaction, in time seeing his tiny eyebrows and lips move to mimic what he was seeing. With his first smile, I was hooked. Whatever would cause that fleeting smile to appear, I would repeat, largely to the amusement of those around me. I also clearly recall the rhythm of what he found comforting. When he was upset he wanted to be held and rocked with a simultaneous swaying and bouncing motion. This could not be achieved while sitting, but rather required walking around the room. Step, sway, bounce; step, sway, bounce. He wanted maximum motion in our mother-son waltz.

His father was quite the expert baby-dancer himself. When I was barely home from the hospital, still recovering from my emergency c-section, I lacked the ability to produce an adequately exuberant bounce. Walking was a slow and painful process at best, even without the added attempt to throw in a bit of "Dancing with the Stars." My husband gladly stepped in, providing just the right amount of mojo with his moves as judged by Craig. At times I simply could not comfort Craig. I felt rejected, probably fueled by a bit of postpartum and post-anesthesia depression. I recall Mark bouncing Craig, who was crying with colic while I was sitting on the couch crying with despair, "Our baby doesn't like me!" Mark replied, with the perfect humor for the moment and his highly logical, engineer problem-solving skills, "I can't bounce both of you at once. You'll need to take a number." Thus began my parenting dance lessons!

Made for Relationships

Even without knowing why it's necessary, we parents automatically do the right thing in relationship with our children. If you think back to your own child's infancy, I am sure that you too had some sort of rocking, bouncing, swaying motion that was just the right thing to soothe your child. You too made humorous facial expressions and funny sounds. We are wired for connection and relationship, and these simple actions we do automatically are critical building blocks for child development. Babies have a very small world, but their world is all about relationships, down to the finest of details. An infant's eyes focus clearly at a range of roughly seven to eleven inches, which is the average distance between a parent's face and the face of the infant being held. The rocking motion that soothes a baby creates a gentle washing action to the vestibular fluid in the inner ear, which is critical for sensory development for the integration of sight, sound, and location in space. There is plenty of research supporting that infants who lack these important relational interactions are negatively impacted in a variety of ways that continue past childhood.

From the moment when we are born, we are made for relationships. We are created with a need for love, belonging, acceptance, and connection in the world. The story of creation is born out of relationship, our relationship to God first, then other significant relationships with family and friends and community. Relationships are part of who we are and how we define ourselves in the world. I am Craig's mom, Mark's wife, Carol and Dave's daughter, Lisa's BFF, and many more relationships besides. A person's family, both immediate and extended, friends, neighbors, and congregations create that community of love, acceptance, belonging, and connection.

Made for Relationships, but Feeling Alone

Perhaps your experience was different, but I received no warning that parenting a child with special needs would strain so many of my relationships causing them to shift and, in some cases, end. It was challenging and painful. Some friends withdrew. New ones were hard to find. Extended family did not understand Craig's behaviors. We set strict boundaries and a structured schedule to help shape Craig's behavior. Children with autism spectrum disorder (ASD) have to know where the boundaries are or they will keep pushing until they find them. From the outside, that rigidity seemed domineering. Our parenting was viewed simultaneously by some as too lenient, hence our son's tantrums and meltdowns, and too strict by others who knew the rule book we followed. Talk about a "can't win" situation! My husband and I needed to be on the same page. How should we handle discipline? We had a diagnosis of attention deficit hyperactivity disorder (ADHD) early on, but was it really the right one? My instinct said to keep digging. My husband, who grew up with ADHD, figured medication ought to solve the problem since that had worked for him. (Kudos to my mother-in-law for pursuing that solution back in the 1960s when behavior issues were not typically seen as having a medical cause.)

My experience is not unique. Pretty much every special needs parent I have encountered has stories. Extended family dwells too long in the stage of denial. Close friends disappear. Congregations that were so excited at the birth of the child are not nearly as welcoming when parents arrive at the nursery with a child who has physical needs and behaviors that do not fit their expectations. Marriages are strained, far too often to the breaking point. My goal here is not to paint an image of doom and gloom. Rather, expecting to face these challenges allows for the opportunity to be prepared and increase relationship resilience. Many parents I know say after the fact, "I wish someone had told me it would be like that."

Since relationships are critically important to personal and family resilience, this chapter will examine ways that parents can strengthen their relationships. Maintaining healthy relationships within the family and developing friendships help create a network of support as well as emotional reserves for current and upcoming challenges. The need for relationships among special needs parents is a large part of my motivation for writing material for use by small groups. One of the greatest gifts parents who are overwhelmed can receive is the knowledge that they are not alone. The relationships that come through meeting others on the same journey provide meaningful connections and support. This chapter will first examine tools that parents can use in creating and strengthening their own relationships. Children often lack relationships as well, so next this chapter will offer ideas for parents to help their children form friendships

Building Blocks for Healthy Relationships

What are the key ingredients for building healthy relationships? They are: love, time and attention, communication, and healthy boundaries.

Love comes in all shapes and sizes. Love of spouse feels different from love of friends or love for your child, yet love embodies what we offer and what we receive in all of these relationships. In teaching how to be in a right relationship with God and with each other, Jesus summed up the law of the day with two commandments: "'You shall love the Lord your God with all your heart, and with all your soul, and with all your mind.' This is the greatest and first commandment. And a second is like it: 'You shall love your neighbor as yourself'" (Matthew 22:37–39).

Living in a loving way toward others demonstrates your value for the relationship. Giving and receiving love is the glue that holds relationships together. The familiar saying "love is an action" rings true. Love is expressed in intentional actions in what we do and what we do not do. When we act in a loving way, other relational building blocks such as trust and respect naturally enter as well. Whether it is a spouse, friend, or family member, finding out what actions feel loving to them and then intentionally engaging in those actions helps create a healthy relationship. My husband feels loved when I bake his favorite cookies. My son feels loved when I go to a movie with him that no one else wants to see. My mom feels loved when I call. My BFF feels loved when we schedule a girlfriend night at home making gourmet bruschetta, which now includes cocktail attire as part of the tradition.

Time and attention help relationships thrive. Being intentional in setting aside time to stay connected in a relationship can be expressed in many ways. A shared meal, phone call, greeting card, even a quick text message, invest further into the relationship by creating connection. In contrast, one of the surest ways to remove yourself from a relationship is to stop paying attention to it. In our over-scheduled culture, making time for relationships needs to be intentional. I've noted in my own relationships that if I reach out to a person a few times for lunch and the response is, "I'm busy this week. Let me get back to you," I tend to move on and invest my time elsewhere. I know their intentions are good. There is nothing wrong in the relationship, but without the gift of time and attention the connection is unnourished. The investment in effort needs to be mutual. This lack of attention can happen even in our closest of relationships. One of the key grievances I hear from parents is that they wish they had more of their spouse's time, but parenting and other demands get in the way.

Communication builds understanding and connection. One of the biggest causes of discord in relationships is poor communication. Conversely, one of the most valued parts of communication is feeling heard. This requires a willingness to listen. At times I am not such a good listener. When I am stressed or busy my ability to listen is overwhelmed by my internal dialogue and list of tasks I need to complete. At times I have to tell myself to stop thinking and start listening. When my husband says, "I would like your full attention," point made! Seeing something from the other person's perspective creates empathy. Even when disagreeing with the message, responding in an honest, nonjudgmental and constructive way keeps the communication in the relationship open. Feeling heard creates validation.

Healthy boundaries guard the sense of self that exists apart from the relationship. Healthy boundaries in a relationship allow for time together as well as time apart. Healthy boundaries also keep outside influences from intruding into the relationship. I know at times when I feel overwhelmed in one area in my life, it takes away from my relationships. Work is a big culprit for me, or volunteering. I get so wrapped up in what I'm doing that I start letting boundaries slip and next thing I know I've not taken a day off in weeks. My relationships with family and friends suffer for that choice. Setting limits regarding how much of myself to invest in work, volunteering, caring for others, and so forth, leaves space for caring for myself as well as those relationships that I value most.

Intention

The key behind supporting all of these qualities to healthy relationships is intention. It takes an intentional effort to be loving, invest time, communicate, and set healthy boundaries. This becomes complicated in the special needs family because of the extra pressures created by caring for a child with special needs. When special needs take the form of frequent medical emergencies, nurturing relationships is simply not a high priority. A family operates differently when in the midst of a crisis. Behavioral challenges create their own kind of crisis by adding tension. It may be hard to act lovingly and have good communication when a child is engaging in a behavior that irritates, worries, frightens, or harms other family members. However, even in the midst of living with special needs, healthy relationships can flourish when intention is present to foster those relationships.

Biblical Witness

Turning to the Bible, we can see how Jesus engaged in these relationship building blocks. He made it a priority to be in connection with others. Jesus had a close circle of companions on whom he relied. Even as he was their leader and teacher, he relied on them for support. In times of respite and retreat, he sometimes brought his companions with him. On the night of his arrest, he took his closest friends with him to the Garden of Gethsemane in need of their prayers and support. He regularly invested his time in relationships, even when circumstances would seem to dictate otherwise. In Mark 5, when rushing with a father to heal his daughter, a woman touched Jesus' cloak and was healed. He stopped and talked with her about her faith. Similarly, in John 4, Jesus spoke to a woman from Samaria at Jacob's well. It was against the custom of the day for a man to speak in public to a woman who was neither his wife nor relative. Also, Jews and Samaritans were enemies. There were plenty of reasons for Jesus to invest his time elsewhere, but in both of these cases he put relationships first. Also in John he teaches, "I am the good shepherd. The good shepherd lays down his life for the sheep" (John 10:11). Jesus' sacrificial love for all people is the cornerstone of our salvation. Jesus embodies love not only for the people with whom he walked in ministry, but for all people across all time. Jesus uses clear intention in developing even the most challenging of relationships.

Letting Go of Toxic Relationships

Part of building healthy relationships is recognizing and letting go of toxic relationships. We all have those at some point, that person who leaves you feeling drained or frustrated with each encounter. Special needs parents have limited relationship resources, too limited to invest in people who are draining. Getting free from toxic relationships is part of building healthy boundaries. There are folks who have the capacity to invade lives with their drama and neediness. In advising his disciples about how to enter into new relationships when sharing the gospel, Jesus offered: "As you enter the house, greet it. If the house is worthy, let your peace come upon it; but if it is not worthy, let your peace return to you. If anyone will not welcome you or listen to your words, shake off the dust from your feet as you leave that house or town" (Matthew 10:12–14).

Jesus' advice to his followers is not to get caught into arguments and not to carry the negativity of others with them. Let it go and move on. This can be easier said than done depending on the circumstances of the relationship, but there are still ways to impose healthy boundaries. Evaluate the relationship. Why is this person in your life? In what ways does he or she create a negative impact? How can you use the building blocks of love, time/attention, communication, and healthy boundaries to eliminate or reduce this person's impact on your life? This can take many forms depending on the relationship and its value to you.

I had a person in my life who regularly had a crisis of epic proportion whenever I had an opportunity for respite. In hindsight, I do not think she could tolerate my attention focused away from her. As this turned into a pattern, I began to treat the relationship as a ministry rather than a friendship. I chose not to abandon the relationship entirely (love). Rather, I set healthy boundaries for myself and tried to help this person get to a better state of self-reliance and awareness of how her actions impacted others (communication). I also stopped replying to late night text messages and saved them for a time when it was not intrusive on my need for time with my family and sleep (time/attention). Over time she became less needy of me, and the negative impact in my life disappeared.

Hope for Healthy Relationships

Healthy relationships are an important part of building resilience in special needs parents. Where to begin?

Set priorities. Which are the relationships you value most? Which are the relationships most in need of nurture? Spouse? Child? Friends? Set priorities to focus your attention there. A pastor I know shared that he and his wife make an intentional priority to set aside a few evenings each month to nurture relationships with other couples so that they had friendships.

Understand the difference between acquaintances and friends. Social media announces our friend count and number of connections.

Who can you really count on when needed? Who can hear your disappointments without judgment? Who is willing to work through challenges with you? Do you return the favor? Those are your real friends.

Create space for the important relationships. In my household we have "family time" pretty much every weeknight. We read together or watch a show or share a meal. Studies show the simple act of eating together builds family resilience as it engages all four building blocks (loving action, time, communication, and healthy boundaries). My husband and I set a priority for a weekly date night. For my most valued friendships I try to keep regular contact and get together as often as possible.

Pay attention to the give-and-take of relationships. Are you giving too much and in need of getting something more back? Are you taking too much yourself? Relationships should have a rhythm to them. At times we are in need and at times we are the ones offering support. Relationships that lack a balance of give-and-take become draining over time for the person who is always in the mode of giving. This is one of the reasons that self-care for special needs parents is so important. At times when folks would ask about Craig and his needs I might reply, "Thanks for caring. You are always so nice to ask, but tonight let's talk about what's going on in your world." Or, if I needed to vent, I'd take a few minutes for that and then say, "That's enough about me, moving on. How's your week?"

Enjoy being a parent. Yes, there are therapies to do, medications to administer, schedules to watch, behaviors to observe and modify. Just remember you are a parent and not a caseworker even though it sure can feel that way at times.

Set healthy boundaries between you and your child. I often experience among special needs parents a sense of a blurring of that boundary. I have heard the pronoun "we" countless times. We got a low grade on the math test. We had a rough day at school. We forgot our medication. We had five seizures last night. We have the flu. (That last one always throws me, and I have to clarify who is actually sick, the whole household or the child.)

What about My Child?

As I have led this section about relationships with a variety of groups, I noticed a pattern. While I was trying to focus on how parents can support the friendships they do have, they wanted to talk about the friendships that their children do not have. Being a special needs child can be very lonely. Believe me, I get it! It was, and remains at times, a pain that I wanted desperately to make all better. I have some strategies to share that served us well over the years. My son did not have many friends when he was very young, but gradually was able to develop and nurture a few close friendships into his teen years and beyond. I recognize that this is not a universal list for all the various differences among our children. Hopefully it will at least provide some fertile ground for other ideas to spring up for you as well.

1. In new social settings, prepare your child for what to expect and prepare those who will be meeting your child, if appropriate. Children can have a lot of curiosity about wheelchairs, assistive hearing devices, and so forth. If a child is nonverbal other children may wonder, "Why is he ignoring me?" Introducing your child by explaining differences, inviting questions, and focusing on what your child can do will go a long way in making others more comfortable around your child.

2. Remind your child that every friendship starts by meeting someone new. Friendships take time to develop and you have to meet a lot of people before finding true friends.

3. Have your child talk to kids who are friendly and suggest your child ask them questions. Kids love to talk about what they did over the summer, favorite games, and pets. Be an interested listener.

4. Have him or her look for others who are alone and talk to them. My son can spot a kid on autism spectrum in a heartbeat. Like matches with like sometimes. They get him in a way others don't.

5. Have your child make friends with grownups at school. The cafeteria monitor can be a great ally in finding friends and avoiding bullying.

6. Dress like everyone else. This sounds basic, but it is amazing what an impact it can have if a child is "overdressed" for school, especially boys. If they look like they came from a fashion shoot for children's resort wear, change their clothes! Also, be tidy. Combing hair and getting a bath may be a battle every day, but that is worth the fight. Unkempt kids get teased and even adults comment.

7. If you feed them they will come. If Craig had a friend over in elementary school (not an everyday occurrence!) I would ask his guest what was his or her favorite cookie and then bake them while the kids played. Over the years Craig's friends started calling our house "Craig's Pub." As teens, I started calling them the herd that comes to graze.

8. In keeping with the above strategy, drop by once or twice a month to the school cafeteria with a couple of pizzas or one of those giant cookie cakes. Some folks grab a slice and run. Others grab a slice and stay. Sharing food at a table creates connection.

9. If you typically pack a treat in your child's lunch, pack two so that your child has an extra to share if that is allowed at your child's school.

10. Invite others. Waiting around for a play date invitation that doesn't come feels lousy. Make the effort to extend yourself. Sometimes there will be rejection, but other times you get a winner.

11. Be intentional about fostering relationships. Even small acts of kindness are nurturing. If your child mentions that a friend was not at school that day call the parents and check in to see if everything is okay. Maybe they will return the favor someday.

Just One Friend

I know many special needs parents shared my prayer for the beginning of the school year, "Just one friend, Lord. May my child find a friend." I have been mulling around an idea for how churches can help our children make friends, perhaps by hosting a "Just One Friend" night. Invite the special needs community and anyone else who is looking for friendships. Set up games and activities. Parents stay and help foster connections. This is required. This isn't a respite night. It's a relationship-building night. Kids build relationships with kids. Parents build relationships with parents who are on the same journey. The general premise is that folks are coming to have fun and meet new people that they may want to connect with after game night is over. Volunteers are built into the program since the parents must stay. Coordinators would be needed for activities and refreshments, and the budget for incidental expenses would be small. These friendship building nights might be a way churches could offer important relief from isolation for parents and children alike, which is a big part of healing on the journey with special needs.

Closing Thoughts

Healthy relationships are an important part of the journey with special needs. In challenging times it is especially important to have a core of support. At the beginning of this chapter I quoted a well-known verse from the story of Ruth. Naomi had lost her husband and her two sons who were also married. In Naomi's culture, a woman's status and security was found in her connections with the men in her family. Her worth was tied to fertility. All three of the widows were in a precarious situation, but especially so for Naomi. Unlike Naomi, her daughters-in-law were young and could hold onto hope of another marriage. Yet, in the midst of the darkest of times, Naomi had a core relationship with her daughter-in-law Ruth that provided support. The health of her relationship with her daughter-in-law revealed itself in Ruth's fierce loyalty. Their mutual support sustained them both through the hardest of times. It may seem difficult to set a high priority to build healthy relationships with so many other pressing needs. However, as with self-care, healthy relationships are a key tool to personal resilience for the journey ahead.

Questions for Small Groups and Personal Reflection

1. Which are the key relationships you want to nurture?

2. Have you lost friends because of special needs? Why? Have you gained good friends? How?

3. How can you apply the four building blocks (love, time/attention, communication, and healthy boundaries) to nurture key relationships?

4. Are there areas where you struggle with healthy boundaries?

5. Are there toxic relationships or situations affecting your life? What are strategies to deal with those in a healthy way?

6. What is your action plan for nurturing healthy relationships this week?

Prayer for the Week Ahead

Loving God, we thank you for the companions on our journey: family, friends, neighbors, and faith community. We find nurture, strength, and humor with those who share our path. Help us to be faithful companions to those in need of our strength. Guide us to those who can be our shelter in times of need. In the midst of our journey there are times when we have felt lifted, carried, and held. Thank you for that loving nurture. Amen.

Scripture

But Naomi said, "Turn back, my daughters, why will you go with me? Do I still have sons in my womb that they may become your husbands? Turn back, my daughters, go your way, for I am too old to have a husband. Even if I thought there was hope for me, even if I should have a husband tonight and bear sons, would you then wait until they were grown? Would you then refrain from marrying? No, my daughters, it has been far more bitter for me than for you, because the hand of the Lord has turned against me."

Then they wept aloud again. Orpah kissed her mother-in-law, but Ruth clung to her. So she said, "See, your sister-in-law has gone back to her people and to her gods; return after your sister-in-law."

But Ruth said, "Do not press me to leave you or to turn back from following you! Where you go, I will go; where you lodge, I will lodge; your people shall be my people, and your God my God. Where you die, I will die—there will I be buried. May the Lord do thus and so to me, and more as well, if even death parts me from you!"

When Naomi saw that she was determined to go with her, she said no more to her. *Ruth 1:11–18*

"I am the good shepherd. The good shepherd lays down his life for the sheep. The hired hand, who is not the shepherd and does not own the sheep, sees the wolf coming and leaves the sheep and runs away—and the wolf snatches them and scatters them. The hired hand runs away because a hired hand does not care for the sheep. I am the good shepherd. I know my own and my own know me, just as the Father knows me and I know the Father. And I lay down my life for the sheep." *John 10:11–15*

"As you enter the house, greet it. If the house is worthy, let your peace come upon it; but if it is not worthy, let your peace return to you. If anyone will not welcome you or listen to your words, shake off the dust from your feet as you leave that house or town." *Matthew 10:12–14*

SEVEN

For surely I know the plans I have for you, says the Lord,

plans for your welfare and not for harm, to give you a future with hope.

Jeremiah 29:11

Hope and Healing

Coincidentally the title of the final chapter is also the name of the institute that has supported me in the process of writing this book. I had titled the chapter long before I knew of the Hope and Healing Institute. Divine providence? Serendipity? A confirmation from God that I found a home for my ministry? When I say that I work at the Hope and Healing Institute folks comment that it must be a great place to work, constantly surrounded by hope and healing. It *is* a great place, and I see healing in lives every day. Our mission, "building and restoring lives to health and wholeness," is a fine goal to cloak myself with on a daily basis. One of the main ways I experience both hope and healing in my life is through the special needs parenting groups that I lead.

Living with special needs creates opportunities to find hope and healing in everyday life. To fully embrace those possibilities, we need a fresh understanding of how hope and healing exist with special needs. What does hope feel like when the world you pictured for your child is drastically altered? What does healing look like apart from a cure?

What Is Hope?

What is hope? We all know what it feels like to have hope, that flush of anticipation for unrevealed possibilities. That sense can be articulated in many ways:

"Hope" is the thing with feathers -
That perches in the soul -
And sings the tune without the words -
And never stops - at all —*Emily Dickinson*

Hope is grief's best music. —*author unknown*

Hope is a revolutionary patience . . . —*Anne Lamott*

Hope is faith holding out its hand in the dark. —*George Iles*

Hope is some extraordinary spiritual grace that God gives us to control our fears, not to oust them. —*Vincent McNabb*

Psychologist C. R. Snyder takes a more task-oriented approach to hope and defines hope as a combination of factors: having a goal to achieve, the follow-through to achieve the goal, and a plan to make it happen. He suggests:

- Set a realistic goal.
- Work toward it with daily diligence, persisting even when there are setbacks.
- Hold a genuine belief that the goal can be realized.

For Snyder, hope is an action as well as a state of mind. Hope is born out of embracing the possibility that something not yet realized is also attainable.

As special needs parents, how we live in hope now is different from our original visions and expectations for our children. When anticipating the birth of a child, there are certain hopes that we carry. We may hope for a certain gender, athletic skill, or intellect. One parent I spoke to said all she hoped for was a happy, healthy sleeper. Whatever our hopes may be, wellness of mind and body is certainly on the list. For many, those are simply expectations with little consideration of other possibilities. With diagnosis comes letting go of parts of that hoped-for future for your child. It does not mean living without hope. Rather it means living in hope for a different future. Special needs author Jolene Philo writes about "dreaming a different dream" for her child. Living in hope involves learning to dream new dreams even in the midst of the very real grief of letting go of other dreams.

Stories of Hope in the Bible

As Christians we are called to live in hope. Paul wrote the Romans about the importance of living in hope: "We know that the whole creation has been groaning in labor pains until now; and not only the creation, but we ourselves, who have the first fruits of the Spirit, groan inwardly while we wait for adoption, the redemption of our bodies. For in hope we were saved. Now hope that is seen is not hope. For who hopes for what is seen? But if we hope for what we do not see, we wait for it with patience" (Romans 8:22–25).

In Christ, through living in our hope of eternal salvation, the burdens of day-to-day challenges are lessened. While there is real comfort in thinking about eternity and the place where there is no more crying or suffering or pain, there is also real hope in Christ right now experienced in the day-to-day. A family I know is under tremendous stress with their child's special needs. They are praying for hopeful direction and the promise of solutions. I received an email from a person with a depth of experience and expertise that offered a new window of hope to the family. We feel God's hand in this connection.

Hope sometimes comes in the form of connecting with someone who can say, "I understand. I have lived there too. Here is what worked for me."

Even in the darkest of times, God calls us toward hope. The sixth century BCE prophet Jeremiah lived in Jerusalem during the time of the siege, fall, and deportation of the population of Jerusalem. Even then, God called Jeremiah to a vision of hope:

> See, the siege ramps have been cast up against the city to take it, and the city, faced with sword, famine, and pestilence, has been given into the hands of the Chaldeans who are fighting against it. What you spoke has happened, as you yourself can see. Yet you, O Lord God, have said to me, "Buy the field for money and get witnesses"—though the city has been given into the hands of the Chaldeans. The word of the Lord came to Jeremiah: See, I am the Lord, the God of all flesh; is anything too hard for me? (Jeremiah 32:24–27).

Living in a walled city that was cut off from support, surrounded by enemies building dirt ramps in order to invade, living with dwindling supplies for basic survival, Jeremiah is prompted by God to invest in real estate. One would have to assume it was a buyer's market! Who invests in the future when surrounded by devastation? It takes a person who trusts God and is filled with the hope for a future that cannot be seen. What God calls Jeremiah to do is a good lesson for special needs parents. Even in the midst of crisis and facing an unknown future, what is the hope that you can embrace?

Hope and Acceptance

In my own parenting experience I live the tension between encouraging my son to reach out for new developmental milestones and to accept the reality of life with autism. It is a fine line. Embracing a new hope for him, dreaming different dreams, comes out of acceptance of the reality of autism. What are his limits? Even as I encourage him toward new skills, are they beyond his capacity? Do I push for too much? Academically, Craig has achieved levels far beyond what diagnostic testing indicated as his capacity. He has gained levels of independence we never thought possible. One of Craig's greatest gifts to me was a simple statement he made after he graduated high school. "Thanks for pushing me to try so hard. I did things I never thought I could do. You believed in me when I did not believe in myself."

Temple Grandin, a popular speaker who is also an adult with autism, recently said at a conference that the best things parents can do for their kids with autism is push their abilities and keep striving for that next milestone. How much is enough? Where is the line between acceptance and hope versus denial of real limitations?

A parent told me that she struggled with acceptance because it feels like giving up. I can understand that. It can be hard to say, "It is what it is and cannot be changed," because that involves letting go of parts of an anticipated future that feel very real. Hope in tension with acceptance embraces the new and different reality and seeks the new possibilities within it. The words of the serenity prayer are very wise:

God grant me the serenity
to accept the things I cannot change;
courage to change the things I can;
and wisdom to know the difference.

It is okay to accept a diagnosis of autism and okay to hope for, and actively work toward, relief from a particular behavior or acquisition of a new skill. One cannot be changed, the other can. The line between acceptance and hope versus living in denial comes with the wisdom of understanding the difference between what can be changed and what cannot. Craig has dysgraphia. Pushing my son to acquire handwriting skills that are beyond the abilities of his brain would be cruel. Encouraging him to learn his assistive technology and find creative ways to communicate empowers him to succeed within his capabilities.

As I write this, I have been icing my back, living with the hope of resolution to discomfort from chronic lumbar nerve problems. Even as I have dramatically altered my running schedule and receive treatment,

I signed up for two half marathons. Applying C.R. Snyder's method of finding hope, I have set realistic goals. I am applying day-by-day steps to achieve them, handling setbacks along the way. I also have a genuine belief that my goals are within my capabilities, as does my sports medicine doctor. I suppose I am living a dream similar to Jeremiah's land purchase, holding so much hope for a future with different possibilities that I have invested in what is impossible today. What is possible in the future has yet to be revealed, so I care for myself day-to-day and live in that hope. If gun time on race day comes and goes and I am not there, that is okay too because the anticipation of the future possibility gives me hope today regardless of the outcome.

That is an example of hope and acceptance in the midst of my everyday life with two steps forward and one step back. That's a dance we special needs parents know very well. That place of hope and acceptance exists even in the hardest of parenting experiences.

I traveled to Wayzata, Minnesota, to experience Rev. Leslie Neugent's boundary-breaking special needs worship service "Parables" at Wayzata Community Church. It is a worship service with, and led by, families with special needs. Leslie offered a poignant message of hope in the midst of acceptance.

Her son J. J. is extremely impacted by Down syndrome and has fragile health. One of the many times her son's life balanced on the edge of this world and the next, she asked her doctor, "Will he make it through the night?"

The doctor shuffled his feet uncomfortably, "He is a very, very sick little boy. He shouldn't." He thought a bit more, "But he probably will. That has nothing to do with me and nothing to do with you. We are out of the equation. This is between him and God."

While there is always hope in Christ in all things, the acceptance of God's love for J. J. and the need to give the control over to God brought peace in the midst of yet another bedside vigil through the darkest of nights. Acceptance of God's sovereignty brought peace. Now for the rest of the story. Today J. J. is a delightful young man who loves to shake hands and is quite the flirt, though that may be reserved for pastors who bring him blueberry pancakes.

What Is Healing?

What is healing, and how is it different from a cure? At times it is easy to confuse the two. We are bombarded daily with messages about medications that provide cures. When a health concern is cured, it is eliminated. If I take medication for a headache and my headache disappears, I consider myself cured. Cure relates to a condition. Healing relates to wholeness of self in a variety of ways: spiritually, emotionally, physically, and communally. In the healing stories in the Bible, Jesus offers healing that includes spiritual reconciliation through forgiveness of sins, return to a community for people who are ostracized because of their disability, as well as a cure for the physical condition. Look at Jesus' actions in the following story:

> When he returned to Capernaum after some days, it was reported that he was at home. So many gathered around that there was no longer room for them, not even in front of the door; and he was speaking the word to them. Then some people came, bringing to him a paralyzed man, carried by four of them. And when they could not bring him to Jesus because of the crowd, they removed the roof above him; and after having dug through it, they let down the mat on which the paralytic lay. When Jesus saw their faith, he said to the paralytic, "Son, your sins are forgiven." Now some of the scribes were sitting there, questioning in their hearts, "Why does this fellow speak in this way? It is blasphemy! Who can forgive sins but God alone?" At once Jesus perceived in his spirit that they were discussing these questions among themselves; and he said to them, "Why do you raise such questions in your hearts? Which is easier, to say to the paralytic, 'Your sins are forgiven,' or to say, 'Stand up and take your mat and walk'? But so that you may know that the Son of Man has authority on earth to forgive sins"—he said to the paralytic— "I say to you, stand up, take your mat and go to your home" (Mark 2:1–11).

It is worth noting that Jesus' actions had nothing to do with the faith of the individual with paralysis. Also, what he offered foremost was healing. He offered reconciliation through forgiveness of sin, making the man "whole" in the way that matters most. The cure that Jesus gave was merely proof of the spiritual healing. Healing and cure are separate. In each of the healing stories in the Bible, in addition to a cure, the individual is rejoined to community and reconciled to God through forgiveness of sins. They are fully renewed in many ways, of which the physical cure is but one expression.

Experiencing Healing

What does healing look like apart from a cure? My son struggled socially and academically throughout his childhood and teen years. He tried very hard, but it seemed everything was an uphill battle. One day in his frustration he shouted angrily, "Why did God make me this way? Does God think I like being a freak? I pray to be different and nothing changes."

Hard words for a mom to hear.

We sat together and talked about how we had experienced God along the journey with Asperger syndrome. In elementary school, isolated and friendless, Craig was bullied and chronically depressed. At the time of our conversation he had a small circle of close friends. Real friends who liked Craig for who he was, not just his electronics and the full cookie jar at our house. For a time, anxiety was a constant companion, as were tics that were only partially controlled by medication. He regularly had meltdowns and had to leave the classroom. We both thought long and hard and could not recall when he last had a meltdown. He had not had to leave a classroom for over a year. His tics had also subsided and were relegated to stressful events only. When he had a tic he knew he needed to relieve his stress. Memorization is challenging for Craig; he had to work very hard in his classes. In the process of having to work so hard, he gained an appreciation for setting goals and working toward them incrementally. Craig learned to face challenges and believe in himself. When we broke it down, there was a lot of healing in his life. He experienced emotional healing from his depression and meltdowns, social healing in his circle of friends, and even physical healing in relief from his tics. God answered our prayers in sometimes subtle and unexpected ways. While not cured of his autism, Craig has experienced healing. I marvel at the self-confident young man Craig has become; he believes in his own possibilities.

My son's helping teacher Jackie offered me a gift that led toward acceptance and healing. Toward the end of first grade we were talking after school one day when I picked up Craig. She was hoping for a child of her own. She told me that she wished she had a boy just like Craig. I commented something about raising a boy is a lot of fun. She said, "No. You aren't hearing me. I want a boy exactly like him. He's amazing!" It was a healing balm for a hurting mother's heart to know that a person who spent all day every day with my child was undaunted by behaviors and learning differences, loving him and accepting him for himself.

Called and Equipped

Many years ago I was out shopping with girlfriends on a much-needed getaway weekend. A clerk dropped into my shopping bag a small card with a message from the prophet Jeremiah: "For surely I know the plans I have for you, says the Lord, plans for your welfare and not for harm, to give you a future with hope" (Jeremiah 29:11). I needed to hear that so much that day. I put the card in a small frame on my refrigerator, reading it every day. The simple reminder that God's unrevealed future was filled with hope gave me hope when I needed it most. There were so many days when my patience was thin, or when I felt discouraged, or when I felt like I was not nearly enough.

I love being a parent. I am grateful for receiving the gift of raising a child. There is tremendous hope and blessing in that. Learning to trust God in the midst of that journey has grown my faith in ways I never imagined. What God has called me to do, God has also equipped me to do, even though I did not always see it. In dark times, God brought me companionship and hope. In times of uncertainty, God revealed a path. In times of challenging behaviors, God provided relief.

Perfection Is Over-rated

Ours is not a perfect family and for that I can truly praise God. I tried perfect and it did not work out so well. In Japan there is a beautiful style of art called *Kintsugi,* broken pottery repaired with seams of gold (as seen on this book's cover). Through its brokenness the pottery is made stronger, more interesting, and more beautiful. I think that is what God does through us. God pours his gold into our broken places, making us whole, making us stronger, making us interesting and beautiful in a way that surpasses what others would call perfect.

My hope for you is that through this book and the suggested tools you have found a new sense of wholeness as a parent. They are tools to revisit again and again as grief and guilt try to take a foothold or self-care and patience slip away due to pressing needs. Becoming a resilient parent takes intentional focus and it takes time. I pray that you too feel the equipping power of God walking beside you on the journey ahead.

Years ago Paul offered to the followers of Christ in Ephesus this blessing: "May you experience the love of Christ, though it is too great to understand fully. Then you will be made complete with all the fullness of life and power that comes from God. Now all glory to God, who is able, through his mighty power at work within us, to accomplish infinitely more than we might ask or think" (Ephesians 3:19–20 *NLT*).

While the love of Christ is too great to comprehend fully, it sustains us and strengthens us in accomplishing more than we ever thought possible. It fills us with hope for a future we cannot see. God blesses us in more ways than we know. Through God's love and grace we can accomplish infinitely more than we could dream possible. May knowing God's presence fill you with hope for the journey ahead.

Questions for Small Group and Personal Reflection

1. Think of a time when you experienced hope. How did it feel?

2. What are your hopes for your child? For yourself?

3. What are you actively doing to fulfill those hopes?

4. How do you understand the difference between cure and healing?

5. How have you experienced healing in your life, either physical, emotional, social, or spiritual?

6. In what ways has God equipped you for parenting your child?

Blessing of the Parents Liturgy

If appropriate to your denomination and group setting you may wish to use the Blessing of the Parents Liturgy to close the last session. It is on page 111.

Prayer for the Week Ahead

Healing God, we thank you for our children and for the promise of a future with hope. We thank you for the ongoing healing that is the work of your hand reaching out in many ways. We trust in you and in your strength. You have called us to this sacred task of raising our children. It is both a great joy and a great challenge. Thank you for equipping us to nurture, guide, advocate for, and most of all, love our children. All glory and honor to you for being our partner on this journey. Amen.

Scripture

For surely I know the plans I have for you, says the Lord, plans for your welfare and not for harm, to give you a future with hope. *Jeremiah 29:11*

We know that the whole creation has been groaning in labor pains until now; and not only the creation, but we ourselves, who have the first fruits of the Spirit, groan inwardly while we wait for adoption, the redemption of our bodies. For in hope we were saved. Now hope that is seen is not hope. For who hopes for what is seen? But if we hope for what we do not see, we wait for it with patience. *Romans 8:22–25*

See, the siege ramps have been cast up against the city to take it, and the city, faced with sword, famine, and pestilence, has been given into the hands of the Chaldeans who are fighting against it. What you spoke has happened, as you yourself can see. Yet you, O Lord God, have said to me, "Buy the field for money and get witnesses"—though the city has been given into the hands of the Chaldeans. The word of the Lord came to Jeremiah: See, I am the Lord, the God of all flesh; is anything too hard for me? *Jeremiah 32:24–27*

When he returned to Capernaum after some days, it was reported that he was at home. So many gathered around that there was no longer room for them, not even in front of the door; and he was speaking the word to them. Then some people came, bringing to him a paralyzed man, carried by four of them. And when they could not bring him to Jesus because of the crowd, they removed the roof above him; and after having dug through it, they let down the mat on which the paralytic lay. When Jesus saw their faith, he said to the paralytic, "Son, your sins are forgiven." Now some of the scribes were sitting there, questioning in their hearts, "Why does this fellow speak in this way? It is blasphemy! Who can forgive sins but God alone?" At once Jesus perceived in his spirit that they were discussing these questions among themselves; and he said to them, "Why do you raise such questions in your hearts? Which is easier, to say to the paralytic, 'Your sins are forgiven,' or to say, 'Stand up and take your mat and walk'? But so that you may know that the Son of Man has authority on earth to forgive sins"—he said to the paralytic—"I say to you, stand up, take your mat and go to your home." *Mark 2:1–11*

May you experience the love of Christ, though it is too great to understand fully. Then you will be made complete with all the fullness of life and power that comes from God. Now all glory to God, who is able, through his mighty power at work within us, to accomplish infinitely more than we might ask or think. *Ephesians 3:19–20 NLT*

Notes for Small Groups Leaders

Thank you for facilitating a support group for parents with children who have special needs. As I have facilitated group meetings with parents over the years, I have been blessed by meeting truly inspiring parents. We have all learned, gained, and grown together as parents and as followers of Christ. My prayer is for all groups using this material to have similar experiences. Along the way I have learned some strategies that are helpful for bringing small groups together. The following are a few suggestions that have worked well.

Group Setting

Create an environment where people feel welcome and comfortable.

- Choose a friendly setting that is comfortable and a place where people may talk freely. Meeting in a room at a church with couches and chairs is more inviting than a typical classroom setting with tables and chairs set in rows.

- Adjust lighting and arrange seating in a circle to invite easy conversation.

- Many congregations hold small group meetings at private homes rather than at the church. Homes can be a great setting for small groups as long as parents feel their confidentiality will be honored. Other household members who are not part of the group need to provide appropriate privacy for group discussions.

- When there are suggested exercises, be prepared with appropriate materials.

- Provide nametags and a marker or pen that writes thick enough so names are clearly visible from a distance. Learn the names of group members, but continue to provide nametags so that participants can call each other by name.

- Provide a sign-in sheet to collect names, email addresses, and phone numbers. If participants agree, provide a copy of the roster to the whole group so that they can connect outside of scheduled meetings.

- Provide tissues. Experience has proven these to be necessary at virtually every meeting.

- Light refreshments encourage a relaxed atmosphere and promote bonding.

- Plan for the meeting to last ninety minutes. As folks become more deeply connected, one hour is often not enough time.

- For newly formed groups, consider meeting weekly. This helps groups to bond more closely and creates needed momentum for making positive changes.

Suggested Structure

A basic structure will help meetings go smoothly.

- Open each meeting with prayer.

- For the first meeting, go around and have participants introduce themselves and talk about how special needs is part of their lives. On subsequent meetings, get an update from participants about their week. This may take ten minutes or more of the meeting time, but it is time well spent. It encourages connection and sharing of solutions. Introduce any new members and invite them to share briefly about their own family. To keep the process from becoming too lengthy, open with, "Since we have eight people who have something to share, let's each take just a minute to share about our week so that we have time to hear from everyone. My week started out a bit rough, but I have felt your prayers and today is a much better day. Who wants to share next?"

- Work through discussion questions, but realize you may not get through all of them. Rather than feeling bound to get through every question, pay attention to which topics generate energy within the discussion.

- Collect prayer concerns. Some of these may already be noted from the update parents shared at the beginning.

- Close the group time with prayer, including any prayer concerns from the group.

Leading Discussions

One of the key roles for the group leader is to facilitate discussions.

- If you are a parent of a special needs child it can be helpful to share your own personal experiences in order to encourage others to share their stories as well. Keep the focus on the group participants, though. Just share enough to keep the process going.

- Allow for comfortable silence at times in order to give people time to collect their thoughts.

- Be aware of group members who either dominate discussions or rarely have much to say. Possible strategies include asking a person who does not often speak up if he or she has something to share, or reminding the group as a whole to leave room for everyone to respond. Of course, no one should be forced to talk, but this strategy opens a path into the conversation for those who are more reserved. In large groups, it can be helpful to have breakout groups of two or three in order to discuss a question. This allows more time for each person to talk, even if he or she is not heard by the whole group. When it comes time for the next question, suggest that whoever spoke second previously be allowed to go first this time. This helps level the playing field if there is a person who dominates the conversation.

- At times parents have helpful information to share that can solve a problem. Bedtime routines, good doctors, and picky eaters are just a few topics that can create a flow of resources and solutions. At times, this can cross the line into people being "too helpful" and telling others how to solve their problems. Sometimes parents may not be seeking solutions, but rather seeking to be heard and understood. Guide discussions in such a way to encourage listening rather than problem solving: "Mary has some great suggestions. What I'm hearing you say, Sue, is that you feel very distressed by what happened at school today. Tell us more about how you feel and the impact this has had for your child."

- Ask for prayer concerns and close in prayer. If it seems appropriate, invite everyone to hold hands, which fosters the sense of connection, community, and unity of purpose.

- Send out a follow-up email with prayer concerns to the entire group so that parents who may have missed a meeting are still connected to the group. Also, if there were helpful resources mentioned in the meeting (a book, local conference, etc.) include those details in the email as well. It is also helpful to set up a closed social media group on Facebook or another platform if folks have prayer concerns or resources to share between meetings. Special needs parenting can be isolating so offering a variety of ways to connect is very helpful.

Other Resources

Here is list of suggestions to bring additional resources to the group.

- Often parents may not be aware of resources available to the local special needs community. Perform an Internet search to locate area resources and services. Have this information available as a handout.

- If the local school district or other agencies offer a resource book, have these available as well, or provide a sample copy and give parents information on how they can request one.

- At times, transportation is difficult for parents. If a person has transportation needs, see if another group member can offer a ride. Investigate other transportation options in your church and community.

- Child care is often needed for parents to attend meetings. Make sure the church child-care facility and staff are equipped to care for the children who may come. This will require that parents needing child care register early and have a conversation with appropriate staff about their child's unique needs. The goal of providing child care is to be welcoming and willing to learn from and work with the family. Work closely with child-care staff to help them be confident and capable.

What Next?

I hope the material in this book has been helpful to you in understanding God's presence in the midst of special needs as well as providing tools to help you grow more resilient in your role as a special needs parent. Many parents who are part of groups that work through this material may wish to continue meeting after the seven-week course is complete. Ongoing support is a great way to build resilience and grow new friendships with other parents who share a similar journey.

There are several strategies for helping a group stay cohesive and mutually supportive. Start by having an organizational meeting and finding out what interests the group. Social time? Guest speakers? Written material? Mission outreach activities? Check to see what the parents want to do, when they want to meet, and how often. Most ongoing groups meet monthly or every other week. Some groups that meet twice a month build in variety by having a speaker at one meeting and then doing something more devotional in nature for the second monthly meeting. Those meeting in churches may choose to meet weekly during the Sunday school hour. Those groups tend to have very regular attendance and built in child care. Your group may wish to have a social night out quarterly. At times churches offer child care for respite services so that parents can have a break. It may also be fun to organize a family time together for the group. After hearing so much about each other's children, it's nice to meet them face to face.

Social media is also a great way for groups to stay connected. Set up a private group on Facebook or whichever social media is common to your group members. Members can post their events throughout the week: prayer concerns, joys about new accomplishments, resources, and so forth. It helps group members to stay in touch when everyday life makes it hard to attend each group meeting.

Empower key leaders for the group. One person could be in charge of collecting prayer concerns and doing the weekly communication via email. Another person could take on responsibility for scheduling the room if meeting in a church, and getting announcements in the church bulletin and newspaper for inviting new members. Another person could be responsible for contacting guest speakers and scheduling dates for them to visit the group. Divide the workload so it is not too much for any one person. The healthiest groups are mutually supportive rather than just one person being the service provider.

Finding resources for weekly meetings is important for keeping the group vital. There are some good resources available, some of which I have highlighted in the "Resource List" on page 113. There are some great resources available for small groups to use if your group wishes to use a book format for continuing meetings.

I write a weekly blog about special needs parenting. You can find it at www.specialneedsparenting.me and subscribe for a weekly email. It is meant to be a "weekly cup of hope" offering encouragement for special needs parents. If a group is ever in need of a topic for the week, my blog offers a weekly source of fresh material.

If you want additional copies of this book, you can find a link to order them at www.specialneedsparenting.me.

Additionally, look for other resources for speakers in your community. You may have access to an advocate who can talk about how to work with the school district on needed educational resources for your child. Estate planning is another important topic. Expertise is critical in understanding how to navigate a financial future in which you need to provide for your child on an ongoing basis. Other topics could include trends in nutrition, relationship support, and self-care. If many parents in the group share a similar diagnosis in their families it may be worthwhile to schedule a speaker about their particular needs. Keep in mind that parents who do not share that diagnosis may prefer an alternate activity, such as a social time to connect with other parents not attending the speaker's presentation.

Blessing of the Parents Liturgy

If appropriate to your denomination and group setting you may wish to use this liturgy to close the last session. It is an opportunity for parents to name aloud in worship the hopes they have for their children and then be anointed for the sacred calling of being a parent. If your group is meeting in a church and your denomination understands anointing to be a sacramental act, make plans ahead of time to invite a clergy person to be present. In other settings it is also appropriate for the group leader to be the one who offers the blessing.

Set up a space that feels sacred. Choose a space where all participants can stand around in a small circle. If indoors, use a table as a small altar. Drape it with fabric and add candles or maybe pictures of the children of the families in the group. If weather permits, an outdoor setting works well also. Have oil for anointing. I use a small vial I brought from Jerusalem. A local Christian supply store should have some for purchase, or olive oil is appropriate to use.

Leader: We have gathered these past weeks learning about how God walks with us in the midst of raising children with special needs. We can trust in God that we are not alone. When the future seems unsure we can trust in the words of the prophet Jeremiah shared so long ago: "For surely I know the plans I have for you, says the Lord, plans for your welfare and not for harm, to give you a future with hope" (Jeremiah 29:11).

Leader: Because we trust in a future with hope, we will now name aloud our hopes for our children. *(Allow each participant to name their hope for their child. You may go around the room in order or allow people to speak up as they feel led.)*

Leader: We have been given the sacred task of raising children. At times it feels really hard, but we trust that what God calls us to do God also equips us to do. So for the journey ahead I bless each of you for your special calling as a parent.

Leader: *(Proceed around the circle and bless each parent by anointing him or her on the forehead with oil, marking a small cross. Offer a simple blessing.)* Holy God, bless *(say name of parent)* as a parent raising a beautiful child of God. Strengthen him/her and fill him/her with peace and hope. Amen.

Leader: *(after anointing all participants)* Let us pray.
God of hope, we gather today trusting in your promise of a future with hope. We name those hopes to you. We know that you are faithful. We know that you are with us and we are not alone. Strengthen us when we feel weak. Assure us when we are uncertain. Fill us when we feel empty. Amen.

Leader: *(benediction/sending forth)* Now I offer to you the blessing that Paul offered to the church in Ephesus: "May you experience the love of Christ, though it is too great to understand fully. Then you will be made complete with all the fullness of life and power that comes from God. Now all glory to God, who is able, through his mighty power at work within us, to accomplish infinitely more than we might ask or think" (Ephesians 3:19–20 *NLT*).

Resource List

Ongoing Special Needs Parent Support

Sandra Peoples and Lee Peoples, Jr.

Held: Learning to Live in God's Grip: A Bible Study for Special-Needs Parents

Speechless: Finding God's Grace in My Son's Autism

Jolene Philo

A Different Dream for My Child: Meditations for Parents of Critically or Chronically Ill Children

Different Dream Parenting: A Practical Guide to Raising a Child with Special Needs

Kathleen Deyer Bolduc

The Spiritual Art of Raising Children with Disabilities

His Name Is Joel: Searching for God in a Son's Disability

Autism & Alleluias

Emily Colson

Dancing with Max: A Mother and Son Who Broke Free

Karen Jackson

Loving Samantha: Stories of Families and Friends, Faith, Love, and Community in a World that Includes Autism and Special Needs

Jeff Davidson

No More Peanut Butter Sandwiches: A Father, A Son with Special Needs, and Their Journey with God

General Special Needs Parenting

Jolene Philo

The Caregiver's Notebook: An Organizational Tool and Support to Help You Care for Others

Don Meyer and David Gallagher

The Sibling Slam Book: What It's Really Like To Have a Brother or Sister with Special Needs

Tools for Churches to Begin Special Needs Ministries

Leslie Neugent

Red Fish Theology, Parables: a How-to Guide for Offering a Radically Inclusive Worship Service with the Special Needs Community

Katie Wetherbee and Jolene Philo

Every Child Welcome: A Menu of Strategies for Including Kids with Special Needs

Amy Fenton Lee

Leading a Special Needs Ministry: A Practical Guide to Including Children and Loving Families

Erik Carter

Including People with Disabilities in Faith Communities: A Guide for Service Providers, Families, and Congregations

Kathleen Bolduc

A Place Called Acceptance: Ministry with Families of Children with Disabilities

Don Meyer

Sibshops: Workshops for Siblings of Children with Special Needs, Revised Edition

Charting the Life Course: A Guide for Individuals, Families and Professionals (search at www.mofamilytofamily.org)

Note from the Author

I write a weekly blog about special needs parenting. You can subscribe to this weekly devotion, read previous blogs, and find additional information at www.specialneedsparenting.me.

Self-care Inventory

Self-care inventories (physical, emotional, and spiritual) are discussed in chapter 5 beginning on page 64 under "Engaging in Self-care."

Physical Self-care	I already do this regularly	High interest	Moderate interest	Low interest	No interest
Get adequate sleep					
Plan a "sleep in" day					
Take a 10 minute rest					
Eat a balanced diet					
Try a new food					
Choose healthy snacks					
Drink plenty of water					
Exercise					
Go for a walk					
Take stretch breaks					
Schedule time to relax					
Take a hot bath					
Get an annual flu shot					
See doctor as needed					
Avoid over consumption					

Emotional Self-care	I already do this regularly	High interest	Moderate interest	Low interest	No interest
Be mindful of emotions					
Nurture friendships					
Spend time in prayer					
Enjoy time with my child					
Schedule family time					
Pay attention to self-talk					
Set aside time for myself					
Find ways to reduce stress					
Engage in favorite hobbies					
Practice gratitude					
Keep a journal					
Join a support group					
Talk to a counselor					

Spiritual Self-care	I already do this regularly	High interest	Moderate interest	Low interest	No interest
Prayer/meditation					
Study of scripture					
Journaling					
Silence/listening					
Fasting					
Solitude					
Simplicity					
Submission					
Worship					
Service					
Community					

ABOUT THE AUTHOR

Rev. Dr. Lorna Bradley, an ordained deacon in the United Methodist Church, received MTS and DMin degrees from Perkins School of Theology. Her DMin project examines how churches can provide a holistic welcome to families raising children with special needs by meeting the emotional and spiritual needs within the entire family. As a Fellow at the Hope and Healing Institute in Houston, Texas, she develops resources for special needs parent support. She has also led parent support groups for more than five years and worked in welcoming ministries for ten years. She and her husband of thirty years have an adult son with Asperger's. Lorna enjoys spending time with her family, entertaining, traveling, scuba diving, and running.